A Gallery of
Recuperation

A Gallery of Recuperation

Recuperation

On the Merits of Slandering Charlatans, Swindlers, and Frauds

Jaime Semprún

translated and with an introduction by Eric-John Russell

The MIT Press / Cambridge, Massachusetts / London, England

Originally published in French as *Précis de recuperation* © 1975 Éditions Ivrea

Cet ouvrage a bénéficié du Programme d'aide à la publication de l'Institut français.

This work received support from the Institut français.

The MIT Press would like to thank the anonymous peer reviewers who provided comments on drafts of this book. The generous work of academic experts is essential for establishing the authority and quality of our publications. We acknowledge with gratitude the contributions of these otherwise uncredited readers.

This book was set in Arnhem Pro by New Best-set Typesetters Ltd. Printed and bound in the United States of America.

Library of Congress Cataloging-in-Publication Data

Names: Semprun, Jaime, author. | Russell, Eric-John, translator.
Title: A gallery of recuperation : on the merits of slandering charlatans, swindlers, and frauds / Jaime Semprún ; translated by Eric-John Russell.
Other titles: Précis de récupération. English
Description: Cambridge, Massachusetts : The MIT Press, 2023. | Includes bibliographical references.
Identifiers: LCCN 2022037252 (print) | LCCN 2022037253 (ebook) | ISBN 9780262546171 (paperback) | ISBN 9780262375276 (epub) | ISBN 9780262375269 (pdf)
Subjects: LCSH: Radicalism—Philosophy. | Cooptation. | Revolutions—Philosophy. | Internationale situationniste—Influence. | General Strike, France, 1968—Influence. | Intellectuals—France—Political and social views—History—20th century. | France—Intellectual life—History—20th century.
Classification: LCC HN380.R3 S467 2023 (print) | LCC HN380.R3 (ebook) | DDC 303.48/4—dc23/eng/20220923
LC record available at https://lccn.loc.gov/2022037252
LC ebook record available at https://lccn.loc.gov/2022037253

10 9 8 7 6 5 4 3 2 1

Contents

By This Sign Thou Shalt Conquer: An Introduction to the
English Translation of *A Gallery of Recuperation* / **vii**

A Gallery of Recuperation / 1

Preface / 3
Recuperation in France since 1968 / 7
**Small Dictionary of the Great Names of
Recuperation** / 33

Notes / **117**

By This Sign Thou Shalt Conquer: An Introduction to the English Translation of *A Gallery of Recuperation*

Eric-John Russell

I ceased in the year 1764 to believe that one can convince
    one's opponents with arguments printed in books.
It is not to do that, therefore, that I have taken up my pen, but
    merely so as to annoy them,
and to bestow strength and courage on those on our side,
and to make it known to the others that they have not
    convinced *us*.
—Georg Christoph Lichtenberg

Everyone today longs for recuperation. In an era of plague and pandemic, the appeal for recovery and restoration—of antibodies no less than supply chains—carries with it the return of more than what it says. Recuperation is always the injunction to *get back to work*. At the same time, there is no shortage of words today whose resonance rings hollow, whose credible meaning erodes with each passing hour. Some are always already subject to recuperation, firmly in the hands of market forces or as parlance for lubricating racket milieus both political and professional, neutralized as technical devices of commercial nomenclature, "straight talk" advertising or community policing—and the term *recuperation* itself is no exception.

It seems like a lifetime ago that the language of domination was defined by a program for "unambiguous signals and instantaneous binary classification."[1] Now, however, a parodic ambiguity, no less harsh, saturates every nominalistic turn of phrase. Precision gives way to pleonastic flux. Whereas previously, the porosity of words and their lack of fixity stood as a critique of language in the service of our enemies, today those very efforts at untethering language have muscled their way as contemporary ideology. *Recuperation* has become what Mustapha Khayati would have called a "captive word"—a unit of language whose social truth is permanent falsification. It is a sociolinguistic diagnosis that bespeaks the way in which the thesis of nominalism, archetype of bourgeois thinking and the common sense of buyers and sellers, denies existing universals in favor of monadic particulars as the exclusive principle of reality:

From words to ideas is only a step—a step always taken by power and its theorists. All theories of language, from the simple-minded mysticism of Being to the supreme (oppressive) rationality of the cybernetic machine, belong to the same world. . . . This is how it is able to coopt oppositional movements, diverting them onto its own terrain, infiltrating them and controlling them from within. . . . The ideologues of every variety, the watchdogs of the reigning spectacle, carry out this task, emptying the content from most corrosive concepts and putting them back into circulation in the service of maintaining alienation: dadaism in reverse.[2]

The overarching question of this book is whether the concept of recuperation, as described here by Khayati, can be sharpened in light of fifty or sixty years of the society of the spectacle's dulling mechanisms of falsification, with notable attention toward the decade and counterrevolutionary restoration that followed May 1968. Conceptually, Jaime Semprún's 1976 *A Gallery of Recuperation* (*Précis de récupération*) stands as a significant register within such a query, one not without pertinence for the present moment.

A Lost Art of Insult

The letter of insults is a kind of literary genre which has occupied an important position in our century, and not without reason. . . . The only difficulty of the letter of insults is not the style, but rather having the confidence that you yourself are in the right at that moment, and that the letters are aimed at precisely the right people.
—Guy Debord

In a summer 1975 letter to Jaime Semprún, Guy Debord, founding member of the Situationist International

(SI), offered commentary on an early draft of *Précis de récupération*.[3] Debord marveled at the book, which would be published in January the following year through Éditions Champ Libre.[4] It was Debord's impression that *Précis de récupération*—less a *précis* than a portrait gallery of some of the most renowned intellectuals in France during the 1970s—would be extremely useful at a time when the eclipsing revolts of May 1968 inaugurated a period of reaction, an era when intellectuals were chastised for upholding forces of accommodation and reconciliation to an irreconcilable society. As Debord appraised the book in another letter, within it "the basis and the universal interests of recuperation are laid out."[5]

This gallery of intellectuals—illustrated, as its original French subtitle announces, with numerous examples from recent history—is prefaced with an essay by Semprún outlining the social dynamics and developments of the years following May 1968. What becomes paramount for the logic of recuperation is its relationship to revolutionary critique, as well as the general role of intellectuals within late-twentieth-century capitalism. Here we find the central question of the book: What happens to revolutionary critique in the hands of those whose interests align with the preservation of a society divided into classes, mediated by exchange, and subordinated to the principle of capital accumulation? *A Gallery of Recuperation* comprises a selection of ten entries: Jacques Attali, Cornelius Castoriadis, Gilles Deleuze, Michel Foucault,

Jean Franklin, André Glucksmann, Gérard Guégan, Felix Guattari, Jean-François Lyotard, and Raoul Vaneigem (under the pseudonym "Ratgeb").[6] They emerge as case studies on what the book considers to be the most prominent "agents of the spectacle" during the mid-1970s, a portrait gallery of careerism, opportunism, and professionalized apologetics that, for Semprún, provides concrete illustration of how recuperation operates within the context of social collapse and cultural decomposition. These writers, intellectuals, artists, philosophers, and leftists are registered as distinct tendencies of recuperation within the spheres of economics, philosophy, art, psychoanalysis, social critique, literature, and politics. The book is, in a word, a painterly reflection on the concept of recuperation with a set of concrete figurations.

Upon its release, *A Gallery of Recuperation* was first thought to have been authored by Debord himself.[7] This is no surprise since the term *recuperation* was an integral concept within the writings of the SI, popularized even more so after May 1968.[8] Although Semprún was never a member of the SI, a February 1976 review of the book in *La Quinzaine littéraire* nevertheless gives the false impression that the SI was responsible for its authorship:

All assholes! Attali, Castoriadis, Deleuze, Foucault, Franklin, Glucksmann, Lyotard, Vaneigem are pinned down by the Situationist International in this pamphlet in the form of a dictionary.

From the right place of the Marxist totality, our revolutionary gossips with theoretical humor. . . . To accost Sartre as a fool, Attali as a stooge, Glucksmann as a yokel, Foucault as a civil servant, Lyotard as a rat or Castoriadis as a dummy, will always be funny; my God, a *who's who* of revolutionaries? In a saturated publishing market, J. Semprún does not mark his position with ideas, but with his tongue. We've lost our polemicists of the early twentieth century.[9]

Semprún's critical approach to the personalities of the dictionary is characterized first and foremost by that infamously bombastic and polemical style of the SI, a prose and vernacular embedded in a combative voice. An underlying premise is that the struggle over ideas is itself an element of class struggle, and since the 1970s, revolutionary ideas—even the most transgressive and seemingly radical—have become mangled and contorted into forms of falsification and accommodation. Yet, for Semprún, the concept of recuperation acquires a nuance in which intellectuals, no longer simply partisans in an ideological struggle, now, even with the most critical intentions, end up in the service of "spectacular thought," or thought that "essentially follow[s] the language of the spectacle."[10] Even the ideas of the SI itself had become raw material in the service of the world of the commodity and its internal monologue: "Submissive intellectuals who are currently at the beginning of their careers find themselves obliged to adopt the guise of moderate or part-time situationists merely to show that they are capable of understanding the latest stage of the system that employs them."[11]

A Gallery of Recuperation follows this phenomenon and yet goes further as a robust exercise in the literary "art of insult," so strongly exemplified by the writings of Debord and the SI, but a tradition that derives no less from the aphorisms of François de La Rochefoucauld, Baltasar Gracián, Blaise Pascal, Jean de La Bruyère, Luc de Clapiers, marquis de Vauvenargues, Georg Christoph Lichtenberg, Nicolas Chamfort, Joseph Joubert, and François-René de Chateaubriand. It is a tradition that confronts its enemies less for the duplicity in what they say than in what they do. No doubt Semprún's approach, of Swiftian ferocity, won't sit well with those who have forgotten that ad hominem attacks, while professionally taboo, can nevertheless be greatly effective in disorienting one's adversary, allowing oneself to make subsequent strikes elsewhere. Nor will Semprún's use of irony likely find resonance in an era where the skill no longer requires much craftsmanship. It is a medium endangered by the dissolution of the difference between ideology and reality, in the spectacular collapse between surface and depth. Yet Semprún's use of irony presupposes an intense conflict, a gesture of subjectivity defiant against an objective reality soliciting complete identification, giving it "renewed value, and help[ing] to make it an active force again."[12] There is an admirable delicacy to his critical illustrations, both acute and grandiose, with a competent skill for brevity and humor. The discourses of structuralism, poststructuralism, and postmodernism, for example, are all pivoted, through a mix of character assassination, broad brushstrokes, and strategic incisions, to illustrate their exemplars as active enemies of revolution.

Cast of Characters

It is evident that the superabundance of books is no proof at all in favor of reading, any more than the abundance of images testifies to the advance of the visual sense.
—*Encyclopédie des Nuisances*

Semprún (1947–2010) was a French writer and publisher. His father, Jorge Semprún, was a popular Spanish author and politician exiled to France after the Spanish Civil War, later involved in the Resistance, and a survivor of the Buchenwald concentration camp. Unlike his father, relatively established in English-speaking literary circles, Jaime Semprún remains effectively unknown within the Anglophone world.

Semprún's friendship with Debord and ex-members of the SI began in 1975, where he began to elaborate upon and deepen situationist ideas. His first books, *La Guerre sociale au Portugal* (1975) and *Précis de récupération* (1976), were both published with Éditions Champ Libre. The first was more popular than the second, an analysis of the first year of the Portuguese Revolution.

Semprún also wrote *La Nucléarisation du monde*, first published in 1980 and a work that analyzed the development of nuclear power as a capitalist response to the energy crisis of the 1970s. In 1984, Semprún and ex-situationist Christian Sebastiani founded the journal *Encyclopédie des Nuisances*. Producing fifteen issues until 1992, the journal contained many themes and social criticisms reminiscent of the SI, each article organized in an alphabetized sequence without any author names.[13] A 2010 leaflet for Éditions de Encyclopédie des Nuisances—the publishing house founded by Semprún after the journal—makes clear, in no uncertain terms, the continued critical spirit of *A Gallery of Recuperation*, identifying the authors it has published and those it won't (see figure on the following page).

Éditions de Encyclopédie des Nuisances published works by Baudouin de Bodinat, Ted Kaczynski, Jean-Marc Mandosio, and René Riesel, as well as classics by Zhuang Zhou, Günther Anders, and George Orwell.[14] It also published books by Semprún himself, including *Dialogues sur l'achèvement des Temps modernes* (1993), *L'Abîme se repeuple* (1997), *Apologie pour l'insurrection algérienne* (2001), *Défense et illustration de la novlangue française* (2005), and *Catastrophisme, administration du désastre et soumission durable* (2008, written in collaboration with ex-situationist René Riesel). Despite his remarkable output, few of Semprún's works have been fully translated into English.

« À la différence de celles qu'inspirent régulièrement le marché de l'édition ou l'idéologie d'État, notre Encyclopédie ne se prétend nullement l'héritière et la continuatrice du vieux projet des encyclopédistes du XVIIIe siècle. Le seul rapport qu'elle souhaite entretenir avec l'aspect positif de leur entreprise de recensement, c'est d'en renverser le sens, aussi radicalement que l'histoire a renversé celui du progrès matériel qui portait leurs espoirs. Ainsi pensons-nous d'ailleurs redonner tout son emploi historique à la négation passionnée des chaînes de la superstition et de la hiérarchie qui animait ce qui n'aurait été sans elle qu'un bien morne catalogue. »

(Prospectus de l'*Encyclopédie des Nuisances*, septembre 1984.)

« Une œuvre de salubrité intellectuelle. Mais qui se soucie encore de cela ? »

(*Le Nouvel Observateur*, 28 décembre 1984.)

LES ÉDITIONS DE L'ENCYCLOPÉDIE DES NUISANCES

ont publié :	ne publient pas :
Miguel Amorós	Giorgio Agamben
Günther Anders	Louis Althusser
Baudouin de Bodinat	Alain Badiou
Bernard Charbonneau	Roland Barthes
Jacques Fredet	Pierre Bourdieu
Sophie Herszkowicz	Judith Butler
Theodore Kaczynski	Jacques Derrida
Jean Levi	Alain Finkielkraut
Jean-Marc Mandosio	Michel Foucault
William Morris	Martin Heidegger
Lewis Mumford	Antonio Negri
George Orwell	Michel Onfray
Kostas Papaïoannou	Jacques Rancière
Jacques Philipponneau	Peter Sloterdijk
René Riesel	Isabelle Stengers
Jaime Semprun	Slavoj Žižek
TCHOUANG TSEU	ETC., ETC., ETC.

« Nous sommes ainsi, de quelque façon que l'on veuille nous considérer, d'une autre époque. Il ne dépend pas seulement de nous que cette époque soit en fait la prochaine, mais tout ce qui sera critiqué ici le sera cependant du point de vue de la liquidation sociale des nuisances matérielles et intellectuelles, pour reconstruire un tel point de vue, dont l'organisation présente de l'inconscience historique se croit prématurément débarrassée. »

(Prospectus de l'*Encyclopédie des Nuisances*.)

Catalogue complet sur demande, en librairie ou au 80, rue de Ménilmontant 75020 Paris

Although *A Gallery of Recuperation* remains somewhat of a cult classic among the French radical Left and scholars of the SI, the book never made the impact it deserved. However, with this English translation, the book has the potential of a revival insofar as it contains entries on intellectuals who have now, from the late twentieth century to the early twenty-first, become dominant staples of Anglophone academia and continental philosophy, most notably Gilles Deleuze, Michel Foucault, Félix Guattari, and Jean-François Lyotard. Its English translation offers the distinctive opportunity to redeem the book from its obscurity, by making an intervention on what today amounts to commanding intellectual trends precisely *within* the Anglophone world.[15]

Yet not all the names will ring familiar to Anglophone readers. Here we first encounter economist and technocrat Jacques Attali, special advisor to Socialist Party (PS) President François Mitterrand during the 1980s, a period that, without coincidence, saw the thrice devaluation of the franc within three years. During the 1990s, Attali would become president of the European Bank for Reconstruction and Development, initiating the financial integration of Eastern post-communist regimes through multilateral lending and privatization schemes; he soon became embroiled in a number of scandals on the organization's misuse of funds, resulting in his resignation. Concomitant media disgrace followed Attali's scholarly work, with repeated charges of plagiarism stemming from the fact that his strongest voice was not his own, but derivative of outsourcing to sloppy assistants. Attali was a frequent object of humorous ridicule in Debord's private correspondence from the 1980s, a sort of exemplar, along with Jean Baudrillard, who appropriates situationist ideas without the pressure of needing to understand them.

Thereafter we discover Cornelius Castoriadis, a seemingly unlikely candidate. During the period of Marxism's annexation by Stalinism in France, there remained one small group of thinkers since 1946 that sought to separate Marxism from its identification with the Soviet Union. Existing in virtual obscurity until the mid-1950s, the anti-state and council-communist journal *Socialisme ou Barbarie*, founded by Castoriadis and Claude Lefort, vehemently rejected Stalinist bureaucracy and remained the single communist publication in France since 1949 consistently hostile to the orthodoxy and authoritarianism of the USSR, opposed to both Western capitalism and Eastern state socialism, the latter of which it emphasized to be no less a class society than its Western counterpart. For Socialisme ou Barbarie, there was a line of necessity between Stalinism and Lenin's theory of the vanguard, both of which rested on the objectification of the proletariat as a passive receptacle for social transformation and in the domination of the proletariat by its own representation. It was alongside these criticisms that Socialisme ou Barbarie appropriated elements of the Dutch-German tradition of council-communism. Starting in the 1960s, the group, now including Lyotard and Pierre Souyri, began to expand the concept of revolutionary self-management (*autogestion*) outside the sphere of production and into the totality of everyday life. While Socialisme ou Barbarie was largely neglected by the French Left prior to 1956, after the crushing of the Hungarian uprising, its attacks upon the Marxism of the USSR and its corresponding theory of workers' self-management gained greater traction.

Debord himself participated briefly between 1960 and 1961 in Socialisme ou Barbarie and its political wing, Pouvoir Ouvrier. It remained one of the few political organizations that exerted some momentary influence on the SI, specifically the group's critical account of the vanguardism of Marxism-Leninism and the bureaucratic state capitalism of the Eastern Bloc as a variation on its Western reciprocate. However, despite these insights, the SI would come to criticize the group's image of the political militant and its activism, based on Debord's own experience within Socialisme ou Barbarie, wherein a division of labor split leading theoreticians from rank-and-file members. Despite the group's critique of hierarchical relations between *dirigeant* and *executant*, the SI criticized the internal specialization of militants operative within its organizing.[16]

In another entry, Semprún unveils the true identity of Jean Franklin, a writer and philosopher whose literary career is marked by a chameleon pattern of pseudonyms. Semprún unmasks him here as François George. Close with Jean-Paul Sartre and André Gorz, George was a managing editor for *Les Temps Modernes* and a journalist at *Nouvel Observateur*. Both he and his brother, Jean-Pierre George, applied for membership to the SI in 1965 and were unanimously rejected. Yet earlier in the year, both George and his brother published *Autopsie de Dieu* and *L'Illusion tragique illustrée*, two books very much appreciated by the SI. As Debord describes in a letter to Khayati in June, "J.-P. and François George are, quite simply, situationists, as everything in their books shows."[17] Issue 10 of *Internationale situationniste*, published the following year, includes the essay "Sur deux livres et leurs auteurs," which at first defends the books as having addressed some of the problems advanced by the SI. Yet the denial of George's membership is explained in the second half:

We did not have to discuss the degrees of talent—and even less, obviously, the theoretical content—of their works, but their *ability* to think and live by themselves. From July onwards, we had to stop listening to François George, who was boring everyone. He displayed the most obvious inability to make the slightest use of the concepts and lifestyle to which his *Autopsie de Dieu* had given a favorable press. Such coverage can in no way suffice to seduce us or to make its bearers interesting. . . . Fundamentally unsuited to dialogue, because stupidly afraid in the face of all that life has to offer as well as prematurely embittered by his intellectual and theoretical shortcomings, François George would have been reduced to run-of-the-mill discipleship, subject, despite his claims otherwise, to a one-sided learning. But this runs entirely counter to our aims and tastes. Whether the disciple wants to hear it respectfully or quibble childishly, such learning has no support whatsoever among the Situationists.[18]

It is not tangential to linger on this particular anecdote, insofar as its emphasis on the danger of situationist disciples remains a central contextual component of *A Gallery of Recuperation*. Although the broad historical background of France in the 1970s will receive greater attention below, it can here be remarked that part of Semprún's intention was to combat the tendency of certain intellectuals, students, and fellow travelers to adopt merely the vernacular and posture of the SI. Here we find the figure of the *pro-situ*: custodian and careerist of the mere *image* of SI activity, its enthusiastically mimetic spectacularization, a "French disease" that had begun to be exported internationally. As a sort of culinary situationism, the *pro-situ* assumed the "appearance of the SI's theory become ideology."[19] Even inside the SI, this milieu advanced the organization's inertia, a *contemplative* participation whose claim to revolutionary activity did not exceed its formal membership.

Related to this development is the appearance of Semprún's final entry: ex-situationist Raoul Vaneigem (under his adopted pseudonym "Ratgeb"), author of *The Revolution of Everyday Life* and collaborator within the SI. Yet in the SI's 1972 account of its own timely self-dissolution, Vaneigem—who resigned from the organization in November 1970—is accorded a special place within the *pro-situ* dilemma. In fact, it can even be said that there is something Vaneigemist about every *pro-situ*: running their mouths with the words "authenticity," "joy," and "passion" with the utmost vacuity, their lifestylist pursuit of a revolution of everyday life, ultimately grounded in managerial aspirations, is at base a sham. Vaneigem's lyrical breadth had become the hot air of the *pro-situ*, starkly on display during the eighth SI conference in Venice in late 1969.[20] Vaneigem had been growing estranged from the SI for a number of years, attending hardly any of the meetings from early 1969 onward and, when present, electing "to keep up a nominal presence,"[21] retaining his silence amidst a group of proselytes. For the SI, his resignation letter, awash in a false sincerity, signified "the poor kid whose toy somebody has gone and broken exits in a bit of a huff."[22] Emblematic of the separation between Vaneigem's vitalism and his critical theory is the episode surrounding the insurrection of May 1968, in which he refused to cancel his prebooked holiday, arriving in Paris on the 14th, putting his name on a circular that called for the advancement of the occupations movement, and diligently hopping on a train back to the Mediterranean the next day.[23]

Another perhaps lesser-known name in Semprún's dictionary is André Glucksmann. In the final years of the 1970s, when the existential disappointments of May 1968 had calcified for nearly a decade alongside the collapse of *tiers-mondisme* and rapid decay of French Maoism, a burgeoning metaphysical discourse around personal ethics and human rights, and a vacuous anti-statism that played no small part in the renewal of liberalism, began to coalesce. Together, these conditions—marked first with the 1974 French publication of Aleksandr Solzhenitsyn's *Gulag Archipelago* and carried along by the 1978 legislative elections and the Union of the Left between the PS and the French Communist Party (PCF)—produced Nouvelle Philosophie, in essence a mass media phenomenon and commercial enterprise whose new form of telegenic intellectual is symptomatically captured by the figure of Glucksmann. As the twitching corpse of both Maoism and the Common Program of the Left, Nouvelle Philosophie was propelled into the spotlight as intellectuals, marginal to the university and with a heavy persecution complex, found commercial success in a newly emergent, fast-developing cultural press. At base a publicity stunt and promotional campaign by the Éditions Grasset with Bernard-Henri Lévy as its editor, the nouveaux philosophes were quick to portray themselves as censored dissidents. These ex-*gauchistes*, discovering the work of Solzhenitsyn, concluded in a number of works that Marxism itself inevitably leads to concentration camps and sought to enthrone themselves as the new post-'68 intelligentsia.[24] Glucksmann, along with Lévy, Guy Lardreau, Christian Jambet, and

Claude Lefort, became poster boys for Solzhenitsyn, parading his account of the Soviet gulags as a newfound discovery.

A final, altogether obscure name for an Anglophone readership is Gérard Guégan, a writer, journalist, film critic, and associate of Godard who worked with Gérard Lebovici, founder of Éditions Champ Libre. Until his assassination in 1984, to this day shrouded in mystery, Lebovici was a film producer and close friend of Debord. In November 1974, Guégan was fired from the publishing house, along with three others. Although Guégan denies the account, the four presented Lebovici with an ultimatum that management be transferred over to a committee of six, which included themselves. Lebovici refused and demanded their resignation, which they rebuffed; they were subsequently fired. The pretensions of these employees, assuming themselves to be vital to the operations of Éditions Champ Libre, are aptly summarized by Debord: "It is always the same logical procedure, that of the three-card monte player begging the question. Have they realized any of their ambitions, as authors or publishers? Not at all, they have had a run of bad luck. They ran the publishing house Sagittarius, and made it bankrupt within a few months."[25]

Semprún's remaining cast of characters will inevitably show their faces at any dreary philosophy student mixer. For the moment, Gilles Deleuze, Michel Foucault, Félix Guattari, and Jean-François Lyotard can be congregated under the poststructural "garrison that has taken refuge at Vincennes."[26] Founded in 1969, the Centre Universitaire Expérimental de Vincennes outside of Paris, referenced throughout *A Gallery of Recuperation*, became a venue for post-'68 student protests and occupations. By 1971, it gained full university status, awarding degrees with a focus on the humanities and renamed Université Paris 8. Its philosophy department was first chaired, with his nascent "dreams of Khomeini,"[27] by Foucault, and during the 1970s, some of its most notable faculty included Deleuze, Guattari, Lyotard, and Lacan, among other philosophers and sociologists whose research, as part of a Gaullist technocratic legacy, was often subsidized by ministries of the French state.[28]

A Decade of Restoration

Ever since social revolutions have existed and ever since they have been defeated, we have witnessed restorations that have employed the most varied methods; but we have never before seen them succeed, so rapidly and with such little repression, in carrying out such a disarmament of consciousness.
—René Viénet

If the characters to follow are subject to any kind of ridicule, it is not by Semprún's pen. It is the times in which they live that cast them into ignobility. To see how, we return to that watershed moment of May 1968, where in less than six months, the seemingly inconsequential commencement of a new swimming pool at Nanterre swelled to a general strike of ten million workers and the near eradication of the state. Against the bureaucratic conservatism of trade unions, political parties, and forces of social democracy, which struggled to impose their reflection everywhere, the proletariat abandoned the triumphant march of the commodity economy and its regimentation: from students to *blousons noirs*, from auto manufacturers, the national press, doctors, nurses, and psychiatrists, to grave-diggers, astronomers, football players, and advertising agents. For those who had been paying attention, such as the SI, there was nothing surprising about the irruption of such a vast swath of society,[29] in which the economic progress of postwar abundance generated continued social antagonisms that called into question the entirety of the capitalist economy and its spectacular organization of appearances.

Yet the elections at the end of July left de Gaulle with more power than ever. The trade unions and parties then assisted the state in dismantling the strikes "sector by sector, factory by factory."[30] Order had been restored and it proceeded through the decade, although not without continued large-scale social movements in the early 1970s, including wildcat strikes, workplace sabotage, conflicts with union bureaucracies and managerial leftism, and proletarian subversion globally.[31] However, by the end of the 1970s, order seemed to reign everywhere.

In France, considerable state repression started in the spring of 1970. The *anti-casseurs* law of April criminalized participation in illegal demonstrations. By June, a number of *gauchiste* organizations were outlawed and many militants were imprisoned, while Minister of the Interior Raymond Marcellin rolled back basic civil liberties through arbitrary search and seizures, the censorship of publications, the banning of groups, and the arrest of militants. In this atmosphere, the French plainclothes police officer emerged, and in general, "the police were more numerous; anyone who visited Paris in the early 1970s will recall the concentration in the metros and on the sidewalks of armed police, the CRS vans stationed at regular, close intervals throughout the central city."[32] Additionally, article 30 of the Code Pénal allowed for "the coordination of all the police forces in France under the Ministry of the Interior."[33]

This repression placed post-'68 *gauchisme* in an awkward position. Resultant clandestine political activity helped renew the figure of the professional militant, most notably the Maoist Gauche prolétarienne, which formed immediately after May with some participants from the Mouvement du 22 Mars,[34] until it had to go underground in 1970. The group consisted of students from the École normale supérieure under the influence of Chinese communism and Althusser, with an overall incoherent combination of a hierarchical division of labor, populism, illegalism, and voluntarism. Its undemocratic executive committee—led by future nouveaux philosophes Bernard-Henri Lévy (whose "iconoclasm" is perfectly summarized by the fact that he spent May 1968 appealing to the educational bureaucracy to allow him, against the strikes, to take his entrance exams)[35]—comprised those with elite educational backgrounds whose guilt lent itself well to an *ouvriérisme* that projected both factory workers and peasants into mythic proportions. Emblematic here is a characteristic *tier-mondisme* that, against the background of Vietnam and the memory of Algeria, would throughout the 1970s fade into a post-*gauchiste* consensus on the plurality of struggle, most notably through feminism, ecology, regionalism, prison reform, and gay liberation. By the middle of the decade, politics itself increasingly came to be defined by a personal ethics.

In the second half of the 1970s, the ascendance of human rights and a new discourse of ethical morality—largely advanced by ex-*gauchistes* attempting to escape their militant past or trying to come to terms with the failure and disappointments of May—came to strongly define these new social movements in France, alongside a farcical narrative on the displaced importance of the proletariat after 1968. By the end of the decade, a new paradigm of ethical thinking and politics of dissidence emerged. Additionally, it seemed as if subjectivity, against the structuralist proclamations of its death, didn't liquefy but in fact multiplied in a pageant of *epistemes*. This flight into individual responsibility, concomitant with the renewal of liberalism already underway, culminated in the 1981 electoral victory of Mitterrand and the revitalization of civil society as the locus of politics itself. Questions of class would largely shift to issues of exclusion and inequality, and classes themselves disappeared from sociological, administrative, and economic discourses, as well as from classifications in collective bargaining agreements. In a word, between 1973 and 1977, *les années soixante-huit* came to a close. "The twentieth century began with Vladimir Lenin's observation that making an omelet meant breaking eggs; it ended with the assertion of the rights of chickens."[36]

Yet the counterrevolutionary forces convening earlier in the decade were part of a larger process of the restructuring of capital, itself a defeat of the workers' movement that would culminate in the early 1980s. With the postwar boom having ended, pervasive uncertainty concerning the immediate future of the entire economic order emerged. Declining growth and a global slowdown in productivity gains, coupled with the collapse of consumer demand from the effects of inflation, witnessed a period of stagflation in France. The response to economic contraction through the deregulation of financial markets, for which capital expands without investing in productive activity, not only proliferated liquid assets and fictitious capital, but also demanded from the proletariat greater labor flexibility and casualization, as well as an erosion of social security.

Yet prior to this, it was the Grenelle Agreements of 1968, the result of a collaboration between the state, employers, and trade union bureaucracies, that initially declared the logic of recuperation with deafening transparency, a nonpartisan assemblage of allegedly opposed interests all synchronized in spectacular unison with a single message: *Get back to work*. It was part of Pompidou's strategy of dissociating and circumscribing the demands of the workers from the student movement. At first rejected by workers at the end of May,[37] it came into effect over the course of the following months, raising wages by 7 percent and lifting the legally guaranteed minimum wage from 2.22 to 3.00 francs.

But Grenelle was only an early effort at pacifying industrial relations. As part of the restructuring of the capital-labor relation in the early 1970s, a series of state initiatives were implemented that would together begin a process of restoration throughout the decade. Assisted by the trade unions, grievance protocols received greater formalization and collective bargaining agreements were negotiated at the national level.[38] The question of social struggle drowned in a rising tide of quantitative purchasing power, recuperating revolutionary activity with statutes on raising low wages and reducing wage differentials. These developed corporatist policies of national negotiations between the late 1960s and 1973 incorporated between five and nine million workers from various professional and skill levels and sectors, and included new national agreements on job security, paid holidays, a guaranteed minimum wage and maximum working hours, maternity payment, training and professional development, early retirement and pension, and unemployment pay.[39] All in all, trade unions, in collaboration with both the state and employers' federations, enacted a *policy of compromise*—itself a form of recuperation without the need for subtlety—against the demands of self-management and councilism characteristic of militant struggle.

All of this, of course, was prior to the 1974 crisis, with the first oil shock and the subsequent recession whereby corporatist policy had to change with the overall decrease in productivity gains. Through the initiatives of employer federations such as the Conseil national du patronat français, control over firms had to be reasserted as the costs of disruption, such as absenteeism, strikes, temporary stoppages, became too high. Weakening unions corresponded to an individualization of working conditions and remuneration, with various flexibility incentives that secured personalized benefits.[40]

The new enthusiasm for economic flexibility was advanced by Mitterrand and the Socialist government of the 1980s. Its 1981 electoral victory took place during a period of disenchantment that had already been solidifying for nearly a decade. Further, entering into an electoral alliance with the PCF in 1972, the PS navigated a Union of the Left of a Common Program of Government, ultimately a failure yet an initiative that occupied the center stage of French party politics in the 1970s.[41] It can be said without controversy that the Union of the Left gained momentum in proportion to the decline of *gauchisme*. "The 1974 presidential election marked the end of *gauchisme*'s dynamism as electoral politics consumed its militants, later to be digested by the PS."[42] By 1983, Mitterrand would facilitate a wave of economic liberalization surrounded by a team of *soixante-huitard* advisors.

§

A final political event during the 1970s warrants specific mention, perhaps one of the most pronounced in *A Gallery of Recuperation* in terms of how, in Semprún's view, recuperators can barely keep up with what they attempt to explain away. We refer here to the 1974 Portuguese Revolution. Published a mere month after it was written and released by Éditions Champ Libre at Debord's recommendation,[43] Semprún's *La guerre sociale au Portugal* traces the developments from April 25, 1974, to March 11, 1975, in which the Portuguese proletariat fought enemies made up of a coalition of bureaucrats, capitalists, landowners, the right wing, soldiers, military generals, and technocrats. The initial military coup of April 25 ended the Estado Novo regime of Salazar, and with it, nearly fifty years of fascist rule, followed by eighteen months of intense class struggle and collective mobilizations of workers' autonomous organization amid a political struggle of elites competing for state power.

The coup was immediately followed by an immense wave of wildcat strikes, urban housing and land occupations, street demonstrations, and autonomously organized community initiatives, with demands ranging from higher wages, firm self-management, collectivization of agriculture, housing provision, freedom of the press, and the purging of managers associated with the previous regime, to the complete abolition of class society itself. In response, the provisional government, itself comprising a conflict between competing forces vying for control—some of which still with active ties to the right wing and the ruling classes of large landowners, industrialists, bankers, and international capital representatives—sought alternative means for disciplining the spontaneous revolts and reasserting the primacy of economic modernization and productivity.

This was an uprising not "against the bourgeoisie but alongside it."[44] The people initially identified with the Movement of the Armed Forces (MFA), led by general António de Spínola, which found itself in the dilemma of wanting to transform the state while needing to defend it against proletarian autonomy. "A pattern was beginning to emerge whereby every spontaneous struggle led to an intervention of the state, thereby widening and strengthening its area of social control."[45] After the governmental crisis of July, the MFA implemented anti-worker statutes challenging the right to strike by giving bosses the right to lock out strikers.[46] The rapid reorganization and modernization of Portuguese capitalism required social peace. Concealing themselves under the rubric of antifascism, the Stalinists of the Portuguese Communist Party under Álvaro Cunhal, the Socialist Party (PS) under Mário Soares, the social democrats, trade union bureaucrats, the MFA, and various competing military generals—this chaotic nebulous, not the police force as in other countries, was the primary mechanism of recuperation, even if the factions were in conflict over whether heavy state planning or unregulated liberal capitalism should triumph. What eventually emerged was a "monstrous hybrid of bourgeois and bureaucrat."[47]

The Portuguese example illustrates the forces of recuperation as asserting the primacy of the economy and the stabilization of state power. Provisional governments along with the MFA and its military units employed parties of the Left and trade unions as deterrents against the ongoing proletarian revolution. With two failed right-wing coups in September and March the following year, alongside a number of splinter vanguard groups clashing "in the competition for proletarian clientele"[48] all pretending otherwise, a liberal parliamentary democracy would end the insurrection under the electoral victory of the PS, fully integrating Portugal into European capitalism in November 1975.

All the World's a Means of Purchase

Her libertinism is in thrall to Catholicism as the nun's ecstasy is to paganism.
—Theodor W. Adorno

If the portrait above paints in broad brushstrokes the political and economic forces of recuperation in the 1970s, it is the intellectual backdrop that brings us back to the more direct significance of Semprún's *A Gallery of Recuperation*. After the exhaustion of phenomenology and existentialism in the early 1960s, Parisian cynicism proceeded with antihumanist detachment and turned toward the sciences of linguistics, structural anthropology, psychoanalysis, and literary theory. Despite its variety, structuralism as a whole held an allergy toward the subject, a belittlement that would momentarily return with a vengeance in May 1968. Yet the breakdown of stable conceptions of meaning, subjectivity, and identity continued apace, and fundamental to the entire template of poststructural thinking through the early 1970s was to hold fast to the continual erosion of subjectivity itself "within the framework of a naïve scientism and objectivism inherited from the French positivist tradition"[49] that gave primacy to the textual, discursive, and symbolic. It is a philosophical atmosphere that gives Semprún's *A Gallery of Recuperation* even greater relief, a book whose combatively subjective intervention cuts through paper-thin opponents in a philosophical atmosphere of having abandoned the possibility of subjectivity altogether.

Concomitant to this development was a new metaphysics of desire, itself a reaction to the frigidity of structuralism, an affirmation of erotic spontaneity against the rigid routines of modern life. This general glorification of the unconscious, and its rejection of norms and laws in the name of a liberatory ethos, would, in the case of Deleuze and Guattari's *Anti-Oedipus* (1972) and with a certain naïve naturalism, allegedly release the creative and contestatory energies of madness, allowing schizophrenic fragmentation and fantasy to become models of revolution. With desire as a weapon against rationalization and repression, the *soixante-huitard* antinomian revolt, as if by farce, acquired metaphysical justification for abandoning *les années soixante-huit*. Lyotard's *Libidinal Economy* (1974) follows this path, totalizing the libidinal standpoint and placing the stakes of social and political thinking upon the impulses and drives. Additionally, the *désirants* of poststructuralism, firmly couched in an abstract opposition between repressive order and emancipatory disorder, were symptomatic of a period of tireless proliferation of perspectives, an interminable pluralism of interpretation, which rejoiced in heterogeneity and differentiation.

It is a central logic of the spectacle that seemingly differentiated experiences advance an unspoken inner reciprocity.[50] In this way, *the concept of recuperation is internal to that of the spectacle*, in which opposition yields a ruthless unity of difference whose conjunctive whole of relations and particulars pivots upon unbridled reconciliation. But it is simply a banality at this point to emphasize how the intense demand for differentiation in the early 1970s accords with the objective and virtually limitless possibilities of the commodity economy. *Critique will always pay a price in making itself heard upon the terrain of spectacular organization*. The spectacle pivots upon a postulate of equivalence, derivative of exchange relations, that holds together a unity of differences, regardless of how loud or unique they may seem, under a reign of appearances. The bark of accommodated critique will always be worse than its bite. Yet if the *désirants* had, during the 1970s, the most boisterous clamor for differentiation, autonomy, and liberation, a better illustration of its impotence is provided by the Cola Wars, an unmatched example by which the unceasing chatter on both diversity and uniformity are each accommodated within the overall development of the total commodity. On the one side stands a product of reliability, well suited for everyone without bending to changing demographics. On the other sits a product that vociferously proclaims its youthfulness, ready to upend tradition and expected norms, today offering itself as an olive branch that would effectively break police barricades. It is a brand rivalry that underscores how social and philosophical problems posed in terms of a dualistic binary between difference and sameness are overwhelmingly compatible with the social form of the commodity economy, if not part of its ontological reinforcement.

But beyond consumption, even within the hidden abode of production one finds the themes of an oppositional Left beginning to conform to new discursive managerial requirements of flexibility and decentralization. Here ideals of antiauthoritarianism, adaptability, and autonomy became part of an employer's consensus and advanced in France by the Socialist government. The mandate of labor flexibility and the casualization of working conditions—with the decline in fixed hours and the increase in temping, self-employed workers, part-time/temporary work and short-term contracts, casual hiring, multitasking, subcontracting, training periods, and just-in-time versatility, for example—was implemented by integrating demands for greater autonomy and creativity within an emerging networked world and its information and communications technologies, where the need to flexibly reinvent oneself daily, in a parody of self-entrepreneurship, was experienced with great urgency. To allot meaning to wage-labor with ideals of sharing decision-making power, autonomy, and the relaxation of centralized bureaucracies and hierarchy, organizing work into "teams" and "projects" with a "vision," proceeded under the banner of liberation of personal self-fulfillment. As Boltanski and Chiapello analyze in depth, recuperation could now proceed through a managerial project of self-realization, "linking the cult of individual performance and extolment of mobility to reticular conceptions of the social bond."[51] The demand for autonomy, creativity, authenticity, and liberation had turned into its opposite, all incorporated into business and managerial practices and enterprise mechanisms, and furnished with a diversification and individualization of commodity goods and empowering experiences, while expanding service sectors of cultural production.

It is within these managerial changes that the militant demand for self-management reaches an impasse. Both the French Democratic Confederation of Labour (CFDT) and Mitterrand's centrism made *autogestion* into an economic force of management and an ideology of electoral strategy respectively, absorbing the rejection of hierarchy and appealing to greater autonomy. Much of the electoral politics that dominated France in the mid-1970s fell under the rubric of self-management. In the words of Théorie Communiste:

In all the current discourses on autonomy, it is remarkable to observe that it is the revolution which has disappeared. What was until the beginning of the 1970s the very raison d'être of the discourse on autonomy, namely its revolutionary perspective, has become almost unspeakable. The defense and valorization of autonomy becomes an end in itself and care is taken not to articulate a revolutionary perspective there—the Italian workerists were the last to do that.[52]

The success of capitalism was always bound to its extension of autonomy, whether from local communities, family structures, or traditional forms of personal dependence. "All fast-frozen relations, with their train of ancient and venerable prejudices and opinions, are swept away, all new-formed ones become antiquated before they can ossify."[53] In this fluidity the kernel of recuperation is discovered, and the principle of endless accumulation finds convergence points in its detractors.[54]

In its very self-description, today written in a spectacle of empowerment and personal fulfillment,[55] capital incorporates an exigency of liberation. Under the glaring lights of consumption, Virginia Slims cigarettes and Pond's hand lotion became in the 1970s accoutrement for women's liberation. Beginning in the 1960s, new vocabularies of transgression were adopted as a commodification of deviance, exemplified by the business literature of advertising firms and menswear manufacturers, against the stodgy and mechanical gray flannel suits of yesteryear. A commercial replica of rebellion emerged to ape what appeared to be an unbridled desire for titillation. Land Rovers became good escape cars, "not only from the police but from mass society."[56] Salvador Dalí literally became the spokesperson for the 610 Datsun Wagon.[57] Conformity and routine were rejected, while rebel subcultures and youth-led resistance were immensely revered.

Against the standard binary of youthful uprising versus consumerism, corporate America fully endorsed the critique of mass society and its bureaucratization, upholding the new, eccentric ad exec who violates taboos.[58] Against the *hidden persuaders* that manipulate its audience as dupes, the new techniques involved repetition, continuity, adherence to a simple message easily absorbed, and, above all, "straight talk." It was a development in advertising that embraced consumer skepticism and made it part of the discursive apparatus, to the point of offering a form of cultural criticism that would rival the Frankfurt School, emphasizing the mundaneness of mass society and foolishness of planned obsolescence. Here passages on the automobile from Marcuse's *One-Dimensional Man* become almost indistinguishable from the copy of a 1960s Volkswagen ad.[59] In sum, no ideas were too radical for the fetish for radical transgression and revolution. Graffiti sprayed on a wall during May 1968—"It is forbidden to forbid"—is parroted by a *Men's Wear* ad in the early 1970s: "The new rule is no rule!"

In the United States at least, counterculture was always an enduring, fundamentally commercial myth. Apple products have been pandered as devices of individuality and liberation, calling forth demands to break the rules and think "outside the box." Today we wade in an online and televisual marketplace of carnivalesque freedom, uniform defiance, contrived cursing, and algorithmic platforms that let "you do you." Nonconformity as corporate vocabulary, dissatisfaction as piecemeal merchandise—these are phenomena that locate transgression, the violation of norms, as internal to cycles of accumulation. The celebration of difference, heterogeneity, and alterity is not set as an irreconcilable enemy or antithetical pole but is internal to the very logic of spectacular capitalism,[60] in which changes and trends are not only poised against static patterns of the hierarchical but constitutive of an endless flux of constitution and restoration. Juliette's credo, provided by the Marquis de Sade, against taboo, to "live dangerously" and idolize the forbidden, nevertheless still holds fast to superstition, to the rationalization of pleasure.[61] It is here that tepid rebellions make great strides as forces of recuperation. The ethos of liberation and continuous transgression of the *désirants* has as its truth the eternally new of a perpetual present, which in turn rolls out a forced and exaggerated flat individualism. It is precisely the *characterology* involved in this burlesque puppetry that is criticized by the form of Semprún's *A Gallery of Recuperation*.

A Note on Ventriloquism

Clichés stand on two legs.
—Karl Kraus

Concluding this introduction with comments on the contemporary pertinence of *A Gallery of Recuperation* first requires a closer focus on Semprún's *characterology*. His entries refer of course to individuals, yet these personalities are best construed as *personifications* of the objective process of recuperation, wherein forces of abstraction have carved individual profiles, a sacrifice of the particular to the universality of the commodity economy that wields personified representations as bulwarks for its reproduction. They are figures of subjectivity at the precipice of its liquidation. Their ideas are as authentic as they are narrow, with only a faint semblance of actual personhood despite, for the ones still living, their new publications, TV and newspaper appearances, and blog posts. The incarnation of these personalities, or "faces of recuperation,"[62] as *Charaktermasken* of the anonymity of modern domination is part of the core of Marx's critique of political economy. Semprún thinks of them not as blameworthy—that would give them too much credit—but as individuals whose structural determination, while bearing class relations and interests, derives from abstractions of the capitalist economy having attained an autonomous objectivity that in turn gives concreteness to the world and that, as a result, comes to dominate human beings as personifications of that process.[63]

At the same time, excessively personalizing a social structure has led to reactionary social movements, populist ferment, conspiracism, and antisemitism.[64] This tendency adopts its orientation as a "register of blame," attributing "capitalist conditions to the conscious activity of some identifiable individuals, who no longer appear as the personification of economic categories but, rather, as the personalized subject of misery."[65]

On the other hand, stressing structures and lawlike anonymous forces risks minimizing the very real impact of individuals. Recuperation is a category within a balance of forces, and subjective maneuvers cannot be imputed to a single Archimedean point for any effective strategy. While it might be true that such personalities function as items of exchange, their individual brands as standardized commodities also serving a stockpile of secondary, infantile gratifications, their decisions are to an extent voluntarily made despite being within a universally helpless situation of compulsory submission. "It would be too simple to tear off the masks and shatter the roles; to cry 'faces are nothing more than masks' is the answer of cynical irony, the solution a cartoonist might come up with. An irrelevant solution, since *they* are that—and *they* are not that."[66] By their very nature, personalities under the society of capital are always split personalities. Neither robust individual subjects nor simply manipulated puppets of an overarching social structure, those who execute the blind laws of a fetishized social whole do so with very real personal benefit. In this way, to Semprún's credit, there need not be any "disparity between caricature assassination and the critique of political economy."[67] Subjective activity is paradigmatically constitutive of that very same impersonal objectivity that incarnates individual wills, tastes, and proclivities. Let us not merely malign individuals, but neither let us simply bypass them by shifting all responsibility onto grand structures.

Somewhere in between, Semprún's *A Gallery of Recuperation* is a critique of the terrain of subjectivity and, as such, broadens the front of the old class struggle into the realm of everyday life. Free from academic unfreedom, perhaps one of Semprún's primary qualifications for writing the book, his intervention is important at a time when so few provocations occur to alert the authorities. Yet an outstanding criticism of *A Gallery of Recuperation*, one formulated in fact by Debord, is that Semprún fails in deciphering general social tendencies in the phenomena of recuperation, remaining within the idiosyncrasies of individual personalities and never quite bringing that reality to its concept.

A Difficult Parry

All this must be decided on the basis of the nature of the living _weapons_ the combatants carry, for the weapons are nothing but the _essence_ of the combatants themselves, an essence which reciprocally comes on the scene for both of them. What their weapons are is the result of what is present in itself in this struggle.
—G. W. F. Hegel

After _A Gallery of Recuperation_ was published, Debord wrote to Semprún in February 1976, congratulating him on its release and offering a few critical comments: "The only important fault that I find in it is that it is not 'cruelly concrete' enough. It is certainly cruel to the authors who merit cruelty, but to me it is far from being sufficiently concrete. . . . What is missing, between the origin and the result, is the critique of the process itself, the work of recuperation."[68] For Debord, recuperation is "not the mythically absolute evil of which the comrades of 1968 spoke," but a "_permanent_ process,"[69] a constant force of counterrevolution that aims to restore meaning and material reality to the process of capital accumulation. Yet the historical changes during the 1970s described above could not have occurred without the minutia of economists, union bureaucrats, professional activists, administrative and managerial specialists, and party functionaries, no less than employers' associations, civic bodies, individual firms, business consultants, police, intellectuals, sociologists, artists, philosophers, and journalists, all of whom exercised their own little influence in a margin of maneuver, overall contributing to a period of restoration that sought to minimize and incorporate social conflict and antagonism—a panorama of what Semprún calls *diffuse recuperation*. An abundance of ruses is involved in both the logic and history of recuperation, enacted by individuals with names and addresses.

There are moments when critique, without constantly shifting or forging new weapons, is disarmed and neutralized in one fell swoop. Bribes, after all, are never too expensive. But the question remains: can a logic of recuperation, or a "logic of failed revolt,"[70] be extracted from the figures contained in *A Gallery of Recuperation*? Although all Semprún's figures are awash with rich lessons on the techniques of manipulation, a thousand particular examples of recuperation would not be fundamentally useful since, derived from a heterogeneity of contexts, such an exposition would explain recuperation not as constitutive of the society of the spectacle but rather as a contingency pervading all social formations and their restoration. What is clear is that the reality of recuperation cannot be explained simply in terms of treachery or betrayal of working-class organizations of representation. Nor is recuperation a preconceived plan, orchestrated by an insidious and elite cabal via subliminal manipulation.

Glaringly obvious is that recuperation has a boundless inventory, a counterrevolutionary force that can adopt a variety of faces and speak with a thousand silver tongues. But recuperation cannot be contrasted with any exterior radical purity that clings to abstract disparity between two essentialities. Any basic grasp of social mediation, as the antagonistic process of an object's constitutive dependency on what it resists, already overturns any dualistic notion of recuperation. But further, ours is an era whose pathos is to ally itself with what it rejects. As Hegel's beautiful soul has shown, attempts at isolating one element of the dialectic while absolutizing another procure a kind of identification with the aggressor. The more it digs into itself, the less it is itself and *becomes* a faithful replica of its other. A theory of recuperation must go beyond the limits of such a schematic binary, in which some creative purity of rebellion allegedly resists "the fraudulence and folly that collects around its edges."[71]

Discovered within the commensurability of the society of the spectacle is *a totally socialized society*, a unity in which experience is affirmed in the identity of opposites within the social whole. The spectacle integrates as a moment of itself all that opposes it. Here it can be said that modern recuperation is synonymous with the society of the spectacle itself, a process of dialectical reversals as a constitutive element of its logic and given concrete illustration by Debord and the work of the SI.[72] The spectacle's "highest ambition . . . is still to turn secret agents into revolutionaries, and revolutionaries into secret agents."[73] Internal opposition is the spectacle's most incisive and formidable cultivation, a propensity that exceeds the simple dichotomy invoked by empty proclamations of recuperation as indistinguishable from corruption. A diagnosis of recuperation must avoid this absolutization of exteriority and idealization of opposition, and instead situate itself within society's poignancy for the mimetic,[74] in which extremes don't simply lightly graze hands but fully embrace and become part of one spectacular organization of differentiated appearances.

Toward a Theory of Twenty-First-Century Charlatanism

The prevailing falsity and charlatanry of this world will always be able to gain the approval of each and every one, but it will have to do without mine.
—Guy Debord

What is clear from *A Gallery of Recuperation* is how the cunning of the charlatan is central to any theory of recuperation. What unites all Semprún's figures is the tendency to chatter on about what they don't sell and to sell what they remain silent about. It is a staple of the charlatan going back to the *ciarlatano* of Milan's cathedral square during the Renaissance and the German *Marktschreier* of the seventeenth century. Throughout, what the charlatan would literally sell has always been of minor importance. More central are the methods of their appeal, their rapport with customers, the confidence instilled, and how they are best able to accord with the wishful thinking of their audience. For all this, the criterion of the charlatan was never the immediate successful sale, nor some kind of abuse of commercial trust against the "honest transaction." The good charlatan, although always bound to the world of the commodity, is found in the skillful duplicity of proclaiming otherwise, even if it means financial loss.

No one analyzes the weaknesses of their age better than the charlatan. Their success blossomed in times of political or social uncertainty, especially throughout the eighteenth century. Akin to our own age, here is an era when so much knowledge pours in from rapid and immense discoveries in the sciences and technology, such that "minds are then overburdened with the effort to keep up with these accumulations of facts."[75] Yet especially since the Venetian Renaissance, new technology was developing with marvels not yet fully understood: chemistry was emerging from alchemy, astrology was becoming astronomy, with human beings not yet ready to abandon superstition in its progress into rationalism.[76] These times of precarious mental security—an ideal environment for the charlatan and their power of suggestion—witnessed a vibrant market of elixirs, powders, ointments, rejuvenation waters, and secret formulas. Central here is the alchemy *leitmotif* of transmutation: promises that poverty will turn to wealth, age to youth, disease to health, stupidity to intelligence.

What do Semprún's figures promise? Attali promises that the march of the economy can lead to utopia; Castoriadis promises that dated sociological observations can be recycled into novelties; Foucault promises that criminology can be wrested from police management; Franklin promises that cultural and philosophical fragments are adequate for grandiose critical stature; Glucksmann promises that contrarian indignation over open secrets is enough to propel a career; Guégan promises that literary clichés of revolutionary practice are a fine substitute for revolution itself; Lyotard promises that following your libidinal impulse can elevate your employability; and Ratgeb promises that the appearance of extremism can help conceal your unimportance.

Only in the most vulgar sense can the charlatan be considered a salesperson. The charlatan doesn't simply make mendacious promises but advances spectacular appearances devoid of commercial advantage. It is for this reason that historically, they were always part of the development of the spectacle. It is not enough to simply lie. Falsification had to be refined, prepared for the marketplace, and sold through a variety of means, such as exotic costumes, comedy, tightrope walking, pictorial handbills, and verbose speeches. A plethora of entertainment techniques, sometimes accompanied by a troupe of accomplices—actors, jugglers, clowns, harlequins, fire swallowers, and trained animals—were employed, and the more successful charlatan denied that they were taking money for their services, instead serving human-kind as a selfless benefactor.[77] Theatricality was central to the charlatan's advertising scheme. Whether they sell elixirs or opinions, their wares ought to be painted in lively colors and wrest applause from the spectators. They need only let people believe what they want to be-lieve while pretending to know what they do not.

The lesson of the charlatan for a theory of recupera-tion is in their exoneration for a social system that pro-duces living tableaus advancing the appearance of no commercial benefit. It "never depended upon *what* he had to sell but solely upon his manner of selling it."[78] Whether through portraiture or jingle, the charlatan was a master of oratorical suggestion and flattery, con-ducted with a cool misanthropy yet with an attention to statistics and numbers, distributing details and facts in a state of fragmentary ebullience. The charlatan's most dangerous tool of deception remains today the spoken and written word, a coarse jargon and droll delivery full of the labored pathos of the pundit. It is not coincidental that the sophists were among the most highly paid of all professional workers in ancient Greece. St. Thomas Aquinas thought it a sin to even stop and listen to a char-latan. Deluding people with interminably swollen dis-course, the charlatan wields terms easily transformed into advertising slogans and catchwords, endlessly

capable of phraseological repetition with slight variation, often bearing emotional weight or eliciting fear.
Their shimmering words may mean nothing, but they
carry all kinds of satisfactions and pathic identifications.

Although professional swindlers, from conjurors
and peddlers of false remedies, have existed since antiq-
uity, a more thorough history of modern charlatanism
would have us trace a lineage starting from the period
in which the tradition of humanism paradoxically lent
support to immensely popular superstitions.[79] The hyp-
notists and confidence men who would emerge thereafter, no less indexed with the cunning deception and
seduction of Molière's *Tartuffe*, would fully exploit the
late eighteenth-century infatuation with mechanical
marvels and the popular craze for automata found at European market fairs. The new deceivers were no longer
promising gold but were now profiting from new tech-
nological illusions, still nevertheless nourishing superstition as the alchemy of a new epoch, "showing that the
age of magic and magicians is not yet over."[80] From the
nineteenth-century sermons of moral and political recti-
tude found within Melville's *Confidence-Man*, the English
soapbox tradition and the showmanship of P. T. Barnum,
through to the twentieth-century ad execs, fascist dem-
agogues, and party functionaries—throughout, charlatanism develops a meticulous inventory of falsification.

For twenty-first-century charlatanism, the *Marktschreier* of today are in no short supply, with every

online opinion strong-arming every other to dominate likes and retweets in an algorithmic orgy of con artists and grifters. Yet today's charlatans are aggressively anti-pretentious. "What does that even mean?" is the index-ical demonstrative that admits it is privy to the dangers of being fooled, and now rises above it. But the fear of being duped has led to its own illusions with techno-logically advanced sleight-of-hand. Although the art of seduction may be lost, ours is a period just as favorable to the charlatan's use of the occult, as can be shown, for example, in economists peddling a metaphysics of GDP, the residue of that medieval tendency to ascribe substantiality to abstract concepts.[81] But charlatanism today holds a monopoly on social media platforms, and here we refer not simply to the advertising companies extracting user data but to the very tone, decibel, and quality of communication that pervades therein. Recu-peration today rarely operates with heavy artillery. Ad-ditionally, while in the past the charlatan might have avoided straightforward reasoning and simplicity of expression, a certain aggressive doctrine of "matter-of-factness" and "common sense" now reigns, a spell in simply emphasizing bare facticity. This "tell it like it is" approach comprises low-key and jaded appeals, charac-terized by verve, wit, irreverence, and self-deprecation, the latter of which is fully embraced by the social media accounts of companies that have understood the ob-solescence of the huckster's trickery of the past. It is a branding strategy of preemptive irony, the snarky mocking of authority that need not immediately move units so long as they are trending.

Yet recuperation today speaks from the position of a groundless stance. To ascribe intellectuals a role in this process, as responsible for imputing class consciousness or having any real grasp over present catastrophes, cannot but come off as a bad joke. The thinkers of this society today are the worst kind of chameleons, changing colors with every change of the wind and algorithm update—sometimes with funereal faces, other times, during election season, with unrelenting confidence that a new era of social democracy is just around the corner. Meanwhile, the snake oil of tech gurus, self-help coaches and cultural counterfeiters helps advance the delusion that "content creators" bear any kind of intellectual weight, while other subsidized intellectuals take cover within insular rackets, internet fiefdoms, and grant applications. Look closely enough at any radical academic and you will find a publicist, if not a used car salesperson. Their allegiance is so closely aligned with an aptitude for mobility, network extension, and streamlining, that a permanent state of anxiety over the possibility of being disconnected comes to define all of their gimmicky piebald discourse. These just-in-time personalities advocating practical reform and political flexibility internalize the casualized nature of their adjunct contracts. For them, like others, accommodation to objective forces of instability has become second nature.

But the impotence of the intellectual today is hardly of its own choosing. The fractured individual is incessantly compelled to cooperate with everything that tends toward economic performance. Their monosyllabic opinions are only as flat as the platform on which they circulate, such that history is able to grasp at nothing that might hold them to their word. With the subordination of thought to the functional order of adequate branding and self-promotion, thinking molds itself to the virtues of marketability, reproducing the socially dominant categories of exchange. We are constantly put on hold while remaining available, subordinated to a reticular world with its endless feed of ephemeral associations and demands for open communication. Transparency of information has always been a key feature of economic competition.

In this context, the charlatan mouthpieces of today mostly stumble upon already established insights, pandering platitudes as newfound discoveries and "takes," a staple pattern of Semprún's recuperators. Works are pronounced as "important" before they are even published. The repetition of a small number of caricatured approximations of the world and half-baked viral memes reduces their complexities into sound-bite-sized packages available for plugging into paranoid narratives. An inflation of commentary and victimological consultancy proliferate, often with some kind of sour blend of moderately polite indignations, priestly hypocrisy, and cowardice in the face of any direct conflict. As a result, the tragicomic victories of leftism are so cheaply bought that they require bare-faced exaggeration to be able to pass for events at all.

While academic Marxists fantasize about Five Year Plans, recuperation today is diffused amid the humiliating "abyss of the ballot box,"[82] the deadening participation of open letters, the carbumper sloganeering of online threads, the momentary grumble within collective bargaining, the symbiosis between woke and anti-woke leftism,[83] and, for the more skillful hucksters, a successful podcast. As always, recuperation is here in the details, dominant within insidious lines of communication and their determinations. If Twitter becomes too chaotic, its functionaries find recourse in Substack and Patreon subscriptions whose clickbait ethos reflects the reality they've made for themselves, one for which brands compete for market demographics, barely able to stay afloat in a participatory cacophony of hackneyed discussions. It is a dynamic whose skills were previously reserved for media punditry, but which have now been universally adopted from the micro celebrity to the milieu loudmouth.

Within "The Class Struggles in France," Marx, in examining the tumultuous consolidation of the various bourgeois factions during 1848, made explicit how "the concessions to the proletariat, the promises made to it, became so many *fetters* which *had* to be struck off."[84] Of course, there remains today an abundance of concessions, albeit less frequently given, pleaded for by those who would assume managerial roles if given the opportunity. Here resides the essence of recuperation as the active or inadvertent complicity with forces of counter-revolution, for which revolutionary activity and critique succumb to spectacular domination, hollowed out and circumvented as a blind reinforcement for the preservation of a society dominated by commodity production. Yet if very little today remains immune to its siren song, *A Gallery of Recuperation* at least reminds us that these "wretched methods" might someday be looked upon, after the owl of Minvera has spreads its wings, as having "wrung the neck of their own purpose."[85] Until then, this translator rests assured that the recuperators of today will catch glimpses of themselves within these pages.

§

The translator gives thanks to Marc Lowenthal at the MIT Press, Jacques Dodart at Éditions Ivrea, and Sofia Semprún, as well as Alain Chaillat, Sophie Dolto, Nicolas Schneider, and Claire Simon for their commentary on the translation. For their support, Jacob Blumenfeld, Anselm Jappe, and Donald Nicholson-Smith deserve special gratitude. The translation would not have been possible without the immensely generous editorial assistance of John McHale. As the original French edition of *A Gallery of Recuperation* contained none, all endnotes are by the translator. The translation itself is dedicated to Veronika Russell, who taught me to never trust the silver tongue and poisoned words of the soft talker.

Notes

1. Situationist International, "All the King's Men," in *Situationist International Anthology*, revd. and exp. ed., trans. Ken Knabb (Berkeley: Bureau of Public Secrets, 2006), 153.

2. Mustapha Khayati, "Captive Words: Preface to a Situationist Dictionary," in *Situationist International Anthology*, 223, 226.

3. Guy Debord, *Correspondance*, vol. "0": *Septembre 1951–Juillet 1957* (Paris: Libraire Arthème Fayard, 2010), 286–289.

4. Throughout the 1970s and '80s, Éditions Champ Libre, founded by Gérard Lebovici in 1969, published historically subversive titles, such as the complete works of Baltasar Gracian, Carl von Clausewitz, Mikhail Bakunin, George Orwell, and Louis Antoine de Saint-Just, as well as the works of Debord and the SI. It had a very atypical, peculiarly national and international status within the world of mainstream French publishing. As a small outfit often operating at a loss or barely breaking even, Éditions Champ Libre had an extremely combative and notorious reputation. Reproached or ignored as a perversion of legitimate publishing, public perception held the project as a business that sought, above all, to make enemies.

5. Guy Debord, *Correspondance*, vol. 5: *Janvier 1973–Décembre 1978* (Paris: Libraire Arthème Fayard, 2005), 339.

6. Jörg Ratgeb was an early sixteenth-century German Renaissance painter. Vaneigem first adopted the pseudonym "Ratgeb" for *From Wildcat Strike to Total Self-Management*, trans. P. Sharkey and K. Knabb (Berkeley: Bureau of Public Secrets, 2001).

7. Debord, *Correspondance*, vol. 5, 390.

8. As Patrick Marcolini clarifies, "Although the words *récupérer* and *récupération* have been a feature of the French language for centuries, the Situationists gave them a specific meaning, which, as linguists note, first emerged in common usage in the 1960s: 'to reconcile, to assimilate (a political adversary, an ideology, public opinion), most often in a deceptive or abusive manner,' 'to neutralise an individual or group that possesses oppositional, differing or, sometimes, contestory goals by bringing them around to your own objectives.' It was a way of speaking that became very widespread after the 'events' of May '68." (Patrick Marcolini, "Recuperation," in: *The Situationist International: A Critical Handbook*, ed. A. Hemmens and G. Zacarias [London: Pluto Press, 2020], 281).

9. Ch. D., "Jaime Semprún, Précis de recuperation," *La Quinzaine Littéraire*, February 16, 1976.

10. Guy Debord, *Comments on the Society of the Spectacle* (1988), trans. M. Imrie (London: Verso, 1998), 31.

11. Situationist International, "Theses of the Situationist International and Its Time" (1972), in *The Real Split in the International*, trans. J. McHale (London: Pluto Press, 2003), 7.

12. Henri Lefebvre, *Introduction to Modernity: Twelve Preludes, September 1959–May 1961*, trans. J. Moore (London: Verso, 1995), 16.

13. By the spring of 1987, Debord would break with both Semprún and *Encyclopédie des Nuisances* following a controversy when one of the journal's collaborators, Guy Fargette, condemned an occupation by high school students of the Sorbonne in December 1986. Semprún defended Fargette's position, which denounced those involved as "an irresponsible minority of nostalgic sixty-eighters," thereby ending his long relationship with Debord. J. F. Martos, *Correspondance avec Guy Debord* (Paris: Le fin mot de l'Histoire, 1998), 211. For Debord's judgment on what was seen as the journal's overall deterioration of *Encyclopédie des Nuisances* into "nothing other than a *literary* exercise," see Martos, 239–241. Martos and Jean-Pierre Baudet also published their own critique of the journal as *L'Encyclopédie des puissances* (Paris: Le fin mot de l'Histoire, 1987).

14. Éditions de l'Encyclopédie des Nuisances later published Mandosio's *Longévité d'une imposture: Michel Foucault: Suivi de Foucaultphiles et foucaulâtres* (2010), a book-length critique of Foucault and his followers that served as a kind of continuation of Semprún's comments on Foucault in *Précis de récupération*. See also J. G. Merquior, *Foucault* (London: Fontana Press, 1985).

15. For further historical account on the fertile American conditions for the academic reception of "French theory" as a European import, see F. Cusset, *French Theory: How Foucault, Derrida, Deleuze, & Co. Transformed the Intellectual Life of the United States* (Minneapolis: University of Minnesota Press, 2008), and S.

Lotringer and S. Cohen, eds., *French Theory in America* (New York: Routledge, 2001).

16. See Guy Debord, *Correspondance*, vol. 2: *Septembre 1960–Décembre 1964* (Paris: Libraire Arthème Fayard, 2001), 82–88, as well as the essays "Instructions pour une prise d'armes" and "Socialisme ou Planète," in *Internationale situationniste: Édition augmentée* (Paris: Librairie Arthème Fayard, 1997), 201–202 and 489–491.

17. Guy Debord, *Correspondance*, vol. 3: *Janvier 1965–Décembre 1968* (Paris: Libraire Arthème Fayard, 2003), 39.

18. Internationale Situationniste, "Sur deux livres et leurs auteurs," in *Internationale situationniste: Édition augmentée* (Paris: Librairie Arthème Fayard, 1997), 482–483.

19. Situationist International, "Theses of the Situationist International and Its Time," 32.

20. Cf. Situationist International, "Appendix 1: Notes to Serve towards the History of the SI from 1969 to 1971," in *The Real Split in the International*, trans. J. McHale (London: Pluto Press, 2003), 83.

21. Situationist International, "Appendix 5: Communiqué from the SI concerning Vaneigem," in *The Real Split in the International*, a155.

22. Situationist International, "Appendix 1," 95.

23. Situationist International, "Appendix 5," 165–166.

24. The most notable works here include Bernard-Henri Lévy's *La Barbarie à visage humain* (1977), Glucksmann's *La Cuisinière et le mangeur d'hommes* (1975) and *Les Maîtres penseurs* (1977) and Guy Lardreau and Christian Jambet's *L'Ange* (1976).

25. Guy Debord, *Considerations on the Assassination of Gérard Lebovici*, trans. R. Greene (London: TamTam Books, 2001), 22.

26. Debord, *Correspondance*, vol. 5, 349.

27. Guy Debord, *Correspondance*, vol. 7: *Janvier 1988–Novembre 1994* (Paris: Libraire Arthème Fayard, 2008), 460.

28. During the highly state centralized administration of Gaullism, technocratic graduates from the École Nationale de l'Administration were pushed by the state as the new model of intellectual, a new technocratic elite that cast its influence in the relationship between the humanities and social sciences, a development not altogether unrelated to the rise of structuralism. Under the Fifth Republic, state ministers "were 'structuralists' like everybody else." A. Quattrocchi and T. Nairn, *The Beginning of the End: France, May 1968* (London: Verso, 1998), 123.

29. "Naturally we had prophesied nothing. We had simply pointed out what was *already present*: the material preconditions for a new society had long since been produced; the old class society had maintained itself *everywhere* by considerably modernizing its oppression, while developing an ever-increasing abundance of contradictions; the previously vanquished proletarian movement was returning for a second, more conscious and more total assault." Situationist International, "The Beginning of an Era," in *Situationist International Anthology*, 290.

30. R. Viénet, *Enragés and Situationists in the Occupation Movement, France, May '68* (New York: Autonomedia, 1992), 108.

31. Some notable registers here are first in France, with the Renault Le Mans and Sandouville factory strikes, Feroda (1970), Leclerc-Fougères, Sommer-Sedan, Batignolles, and Moulinex (1971), the bank strikes (1971–1974), and LIP (1973). Other global events worth mentioning comprise the period of 1969–1972 in Italy—including the Reggio revolt and wildcat strikes at the Fiat plant in Turin—as well as the Prague Spring in Czechoslovakia and responses in Romania to the USSR's authoritarian bureaucracy, the assemblies movement in Spain between 1976 and 1978, the Polish insurrectionary strike of December 1970, the crisis of Vietnam, autonomous struggles in Argentina, various wildcat strikes in England and Sweden and, of course, the Portuguese Revolution of 1974.

32. K. Ross, *May '68 and Its Afterlives* (Chicago: University of Chicago Press, 2002), 63.

33. J. Bourg, *From Revolution to Ethics: May 1968 and Contemporary French Thought* (Montreal: McGill-Queen's University Press, 2017), 63. "The overall tone and timbre of the moment was captured by the fact that between 1 June 1968 and 20 March 1972, 1,035 individuals were sentenced to French prisons for crimes related to political action. In the summer of 1968 the Ministry of the Interior controlled 83,000 police directly, 13,500 of whom were riot police, the Compagnies républicaines de sécurité (CRS). The Ministry of the Armed Forces had 61,000 *gendarmes* at its disposal for domestic service. The 1969 national budget asked for more." Bourg, 65; cf. M. Rajsfus, *Mai 68: Sous les pavés, la répression, mai 1968–mars 1974* (Paris: Le Cherche-midi, 1998).

34. The Mouvement du 22 Mars was a 1968 French student movement at the Université Paris Nanterre, which carried out a prolonged occupation of the university's administration building. Among its participants was renowned activist-turned-politician Daniel Cohn-Bendit.

35. M. S. Christofferson, *French Intellectuals against the Left: The Antitotalitarian Moment of the 1970s* (New York: Berghahn Books, 2004), 191.

36. Bourg, *From Revolution to Ethics*, 38.

37. Viénet, *Enragés and Situationists in the Occupation Movement*, 91.

38. L. Boltanski and È. Chiapello, *The New Spirit of Capitalism*, trans. G. Elliott (London: Verso, 2018), 180.

39. Boltanski and Chiapello, 184.

40. Boltanski and Chiapello, 191.

41. As both a legislative agenda and an electoral promise, "both parties agreed to support on second ballots in presidential and legislative elections whichever PCF or PS candidates had won on the first round. This provision had immediate returns in the March 1973 legislative elections, with both the PCF and PS gaining seats. When the agreement was signed it seemed like a good bargain for the PCF, since it was stronger than the PS. In fact, it turned out to be a pact with the devil for the former, since it would end up losing out in the long term." Bourg, *From Revolution to Ethics*, 253.

42. Christofferson, *French Intellectuals against the Left*, 129.

43. Debord developed his own analysis of the Carnation Revolution in a series of letters to Afonso Monteiro (Portuguese living in exile in Paris who, along with Francisco Alves, translated and published *The Society of the Spectacle* in Portuguese), Gianfranco Sanguinetti, Eduardo Rothe (ex-members of the SI), and Semprún between April 1974 and November 1975. Cf. R. Noronha, R., "Letters from 'Glaucos': The Correspondence of Guy Debord during the Portuguese Revolution," in *Historical Materialism* 28, no. 4 (2020): 176–201. For Debord, the Portuguese proletariat had "gone further than the May 1968 movement" (Debord, *Correspondance*, vol. 5, 311).

44. Jaime Semprún, *La guerre sociale au Portugal* (Paris: Éditions Champ Libre, 1975), 37.

45. P. Mailer, *Portugal: The Impossible Revolution?* (Oakland, CA: PM Press, 2012), 87. While Mailer's first-hand experience stands above the rest, other worthwhile accounts of the Portuguese Revolution include R. Noronha, "A Real State of Exception: Class Composition and Social Conflict during Portugal's Carnation Revolution, 1974–1975," in *Critical Historical Studies* . 6, no. 1 (2019): 93–123; J. L. Hammond, *Building Popular Power: Workers' and Neighborhood Movements in the Portuguese Revolution* (New York: Monthly Review Press, 1988). Semprún's own *La guerre sociale au Portugal* and Noronha, "Letters from 'Glaucos,'" 176–201, have the distinctive merit of locating these historical developments within the diagnostic of a critical theory of the society of the spectacle.

46. Already by May, both the PCP and the MFA emerged as central organizations for stabilizing public order. The former, in control of Intersindical, consistently opposed the "provocative" strikes while the latter, under the mystifying guise of a "people's army" through its radical wing, formed COPCON, a security force of military units under the command of Otelo Saraiva de Carvalho, which evicted a number of occupations and strikes, most notably against post office workers, a TAP (Transportes Aéreos de Portugal) strike in late August, and the strike of shipyard workers of Lisnave in September. Political and solidarity work stoppages were also made illegal.

47. Semprún, *La guerre sociale au Portugal*, 12.

48. Mailer, *Portugal*, 98.

49. P. Dews, *Logics of Disintegration: Post-Structuralist Thought and the Claims of Critical Theory* (London: Verso, 1987), 134.

50. See E.-J. Russell, *Spectacular Logic in Hegel and Debord: Why Everything Is as It Seems* (London: Bloomsbury, 2021).

51. Boltanski and Chiapello, *The New Spirit of Capitalism*, 217.

52. R. Simon, "L'auto-organisation est le premier acte de la révolution, la suite s'effectue contre elle," in *Meeting No. 3*, 2005. Dauvé and Martin describe recuperation within the context of this nominalistic proliferation of *autogestion* during the 1970s. For them, recuperation consists of "the ability of modern society to integrate and digest radical critique . . . the normal process by which society recovers parts of what tried to negate it. . . . Not only is 'law and order' compatible with innocuous critique and inoffensive social experiment, it also needs our active involvement in the day-to-day running of society." G. Dauvé and M. François, *Eclipse and Re-emergence of the Communist Movement* (Oakland, CA: PM Press, 2015), 129, 132, 130.

53. Karl Marx, "Manifesto of the Communist Party," in *Marx and Engels Collected Works*, vol. 6 (London: Progress Publishers, 1976), 487.

54. It is for this reason that the spectacle cannot simply be read as a problem of petrification, but must be seen as a dynamically developing organization of appearance-forms of bacchanalian revel, one for which rigidity dissolves into the fluid possibility that nonconformity is always already acceptable: "Whatever lays claim to permanence in the spectacle is founded on change, and must change as that foundation changes. The spectacle, though quintessentially dogmatic, can yet produce no solid dogma. Nothing is stable for it: this is its natural state." Guy Debord, *The Society of the Spectacle*, trans. D. Nicholson-Smith (New York: Zone Books, 1995), §71.

55. E.-J. Russell, "Empowerment: An Infantile Disorder," in *Cured Quail*, vol. 2 (Glasgow: Bell & Bain, 2021), 127–153.

56. T. Frank, *The Conquest of Cool: Business Culture, Counterculture, and the Rise of Hip Consumerism* (Chicago: University of Chicago Press, 1997), 142.

57. For an analysis on "the industrial recuperation of artistic neo-decomposition" in mid-1960s France, see Internationale Situationniste, "Décomposition et récupération," in *Internationale situationniste: Édition augmentée* (Paris: Librairie Arthème Fayard, 1997), 471–472.

58. During the 1960s and 1970s, the ad agencies of Bill Bernbach's DDB, George Lois's PKL, and the work of Howard Gossage are all exemplary for speaking directly to the consumer's distrust of advertising, embracing the critique of mass society and in so doing, successfully selling more products.

59. Frank, *The Conquest of Cool*, 62.

60. Russell, "Empowerment."

61. T. W. Adorno and M. Horkheimer, "Excursus II: Juliette or Enlightenment and Morality," in *Dialectic of Enlightenment: Philosophical Fragments*, trans. E. W. Jephcott (Stanford, CA: Stanford University Press, 2002), 63–93.

62. In the 1969 first issue of the SI's American section of *Situationist International*, "Faces of Recuperation" was published dealing with personalities of the American New Left, mostly examining Baran and Sweezy's *Monopoly Capital* (1966), Marcuse's *One-Dimensional Man* (1964), and Marshall McLuhan's *The Gutenberg Galaxy* (1962).

63. Cf. Karl Marx, *Capital*, vol. I, in *Marx and Engels Collected Works*, vol. 35 (London: Progress Publishers, 1996), 10, 95, 241–251, and Karl Marx, "Theories of Surplus Value," in *Marx and Engels Collected Works*, vol. 32 (London: Progress Publishers, 1989), 514.

64. Attributing all the ills of the world not to a social structure, but to a specific group of people who act out of greed or lust for power, an evil personified, for example, in the figure of the parasitical financier, relates directly to certain reactionary forms of anticapitalism. See M. Postone, "The Dualisms of Capitalist Modernity: Reflections on History, the Holocaust, and Antisemitism," in *Jews and Leftist Politics: Judaism, Israel, Antisemitism, and Gender*, ed. J. Jacobs (New York: Cambridge University Press, 2017), 43–66, and Théorie Communiste, "Conspiricism in General and the Pandemic in Particular," *Cured Quail*, February 14, 2021, https://curedquailjournal.wordpress.com/2021/02/14/conspiricism-in -general-and-the-pandemic-in-particular/.

65. W. Bonefeld, *Critical Theory and the Critique of Political Economy: On Subversion and Negative Reason* (London: Bloomsbury, 2014), 196–197.

66. H. Lefebvre, *Critique of Everyday Life*, vol. 1, trans. John Moore (London: Verso, 1991), 16.

67. "Personality," *Cured Quail*, June 22, 2018, https://curedquailjournal.word press.com/2018/06/22/personality/.

68. Debord, *Correspondance*, vol. 5, 339–340.

69. G. Debord, *Correspondance*, vol. 4: *Janvier 1969–Décembre 1972* (Paris: Libraire Arthème Fayard, 2004), 460.

70. P. Starr, *Logics of Failed Revolt: French Theory after May '68* (Stanford, CA: Stanford University Press, 1995).

71. Frank, *The Conquest of Cool*, 17.

72. Russell, "Empowerment."

73. Debord, *Comments on the Society of the Spectacle*, 11.

74. E.-J. Russell, "Why the Customer Is Always Right: Debord's Spectacle as the Rationalisation of Mimesis," *Radical Philosophy* 2.14 (Winter 2023).

75. Greta De Francesco, *The Power of the Charlatan*, trans. Miriam Beard (New Haven: Yale University Press, 1939), 103.

76. Advancing an aggressive doctrine of "common sense," the charlatan's optimal audience is the half-educated or semiliterate, half-convinced even before a single word is uttered, fluttering like moths toward the illuminated illusions. Additionally, "The charlatan must be one of themselves, flesh of their flesh, though differentiated by a superior ability. . . . A half-educated man need not be a charlatan, but most charlatans have been half-educated men" (De Francesco, *The Power of the Charlatan*, 18–19). For an analysis of the half-educated or, in the words of Adorno, *Halbbildung* as a form of social consciousness cultivated by the spread of information and the development of industrial culture, see T. W. Adorno, "Theory of Pseudo-Culture" (1959), *Telos* 95 (1993): 15–38.

77. "You two green-horns! Money, you think, is the sole motive to pains and hazard, deception and devilry, in this world. How much money did the devil make by gulling Eve?" Herman Melville, *The Confidence-Man: His Masquerade* (London: Penguin Classics, 1990), 42.

78. De Francesco, *The Power of the Charlatan*, 94.

79. Astrologists were consultants during times of war and commanded a respect on par with physicians. J. Burckhardt, *The Civilization of the Renaissance in Italy*, trans. S. G. C. Middlemore (London: Penguin Books, 1990), 324–325.

80. Melville, *The Confidence-Man*, 215.

81. D. Coyle, *GDP: A Brief but Affectionate History* (Princeton, NJ: Princeton University Press, 2015).

82. Karl Marx, "The Class Struggles in France," in *Marx and Engels Collected Works*, vol. 10 (London: Progress Publishers, 1978), 80.

83. For proof that the anti-woke Left whines with the same impoverishment as its woke counterpart, we need only register the former's analogous patterns with those of the nouveaux philosophes of the 1970s: [1] the state is now taken to be the central source of political and social oppression with totalitarianism projected everywhere; [2] a fundamentally human rights framework is offered in lieu of any theory of revolution; [3] a pathological persecution complex has resulted from years of eroding expectations; and [4] a newfound and omnipresent media platform is celebrated, for which publicity stunts and small racket celebritydom consecrate themselves as brands of righteous struggle.

84. Marx, "The Class Struggles in France," 62.

85. Marx, "The Class Struggles in France," 123.

A Gallery of Recuperation

On the Merits of Slandering Charlatans, Swindlers, and Frauds

The excellent, however, not only cannot escape the fate of being thus deprived of life and Spirit, of being flayed and then seeing its skin wrapped around a lifeless knowledge and its conceit. Rather we recognize even in this fate the power that the excellent exercises over the hearts, if not over the minds, of men; also the constructive unfolding into universality and determinateness of form in which its perfection consists, and which alone makes it possible for this universality to be used in a superficial way.
—Hegel, *Phenomenology of Spirit*

Preface

If there is one argument more persuasive regarding the inevitable collapse of this society than the many books that expose its various defects, it is those, even more numerous, that attempt to propose remedies. The obvious superiority of my own approach, whose advantages the reader will soon appreciate, is that I don't offer any solutions. Rather, I attack the problem in the shape of those who desperately attempt to mask the issue, as with a knife slicing from bottom to top, from hacks churning out muddled extremism to the new breed of state policy maker. Spare me the comparisons: by far the most thankless aspect of my own work has been in establishing necessary distinctions within this shapeless magma, where the nuances of thought are so difficult to grasp that no one until today, among the most well-intentioned interpreters, has ever been able to establish, for example, what distinguished, reconciled, or contrasted the "libidinal economy" of one thinker from the "desiring machines" of another.[1] The many ideologies of self-management in circulation today are no exception. Never to take what the ideologues say about their commodities at face value has again been the guiding principle here. A root-and-branch appreciation of their output is preferable to the output itself. No doubt about it![2]

This is therefore a work of circumstance, even aggravating circumstance. Similar to the ephemerally important and extensive literature with which this book deals, it will be forgotten in no time. In other words, timely at a time when all those with a way with words blathering on about subversion and the "revolutionary project" have absolutely nothing to say about the subversive reality that the Portuguese proletariat has been mounting in Europe, that is, the first social revolution to have occurred on their watch.[3] Yet these voices are nevertheless quick with a pen. They are doubtless waiting for everything to cool down a bit before they touch on a subject requiring far greater application than they could ever harness. Yet regardless of their unobtrusive insignificance, it is unlikely that their silence is solely down to the fact that no revolutionary assembly of Portuguese workers has ever felt the need to discuss their ideas, or anything resembling them.

It is therefore a question of carrying out *in detail* the sentence *overwhelmingly* pronounced by the Portuguese Revolution against all the idiotic falsifications of the revolutionary reality around which spectacular frenzy is organized. Assuaging the reader's fright when I say *in detail*, I have absolutely no intention of dissecting any slight rumblings from the French provinces, mindful as I am of all the roneoed hackwork churned out from Angers to Grenoble via Toulouse. (Even though some commentators do have access to a printing press, this does not necessarily make their prose more readable; the problem isn't typographic.) Not everyone can be a recuperator: you still need to find a job and possess a minimum of useable talent. And besides, the mass of little-known theorists or antitheorists seething with discontent would not function any differently or better than those who currently corner the recuperator market. They would still be hired to falsify *the same problems* that, as we shall see, are becoming more and more difficult to falsify.

I am similarly leaving diffuse recuperation aside for the time being: there is not a great deal to be said about the superficial modernization of all the agents of the spectacle, from statesmen to the vendors of culture and information, whereas the more concentrated expressions of advanced recuperation are far more worthy of comment.

I do too much honor to my subject by treating it with order.[4] It deserves nothing of the kind: any coherence it may display is all my doing. Under my aegis, the thought of the recuperators reaches a consistency never before seen in their hasty and disorderly scribbles. But when you tower over your adversary, you have to begin by elevating them ever so slightly in order to land a blow. Among those dealt with here according to their respective ignominies, no one recuperator in particular deserves special treatment for the ideas they flaunt; even as a whole, their dullness is of an unwavering uniformity. They in fact have only secondhand thoughts, regressive thoughts; and what they conceal merely illuminates what they reveal. I will refrain from criticizing their work. Aside from the fact that it would imply a serious and methodical study of all this immense literature, which I have no intention of doing, it would be a bit like explaining the part played by the automobile within society simply by the shape of the door handles and the seasonal variation of a particular model's *design*. Let us instead go straight to the nub of this quagmire: what these people serve and how they serve it. The color of the uniform indicates the master, not the servant.

Recuperation in France since 1968

Just sit there pasting words together, stir up a stew from
another's leftover feast.
—Goethe, *Faust*

Coming from afar and on the heels of a few time-honored
higher education institutes, recuperation ends up sporting the mannerisms of the little masters who now share
the principal ruins of this ancient empire. Recuperators, who deal only with what revolutionary criticism
has abandoned, have not always been given such short
shrift. Together with Stalinism, the theoretical disarmament that followed the practical crushing of the first
proletarian assault helped all the managers of spectacular culture to prosper: submissive thought could then
infuse diverse bits of its apologetics with all sorts of critical fragments from the preceding period. The possibility
of their practical use, and thus of their unitary compre-
hensiveness, had been almost totally eliminated. The
verbiage accompanying submissive thought thus served

to conceal the possibilities ushered in by a new era of class struggle. Sartre, for instance, with his encyclopedic imbecility, was not afraid to lecture on Baudelaire, dialectics, surrealism, and the theory of Marx.

It was through the experience of this golden age of recuperation and the self-defense measures it imposed that modern revolutionary theory came to full knowledge of itself, to the rediscovery of its past as well as to the consciousness of what it was meant to be. By relying on the weakest points of earlier subversive thinking, recuperation discovered, in what it censored, what was still living and rich in possible developments. Because of this, but above all in order to formulate and communicate itself in these new conditions of generalized falsification, revolutionary theory, if it was to exist at all, had to be from the outset more consistently anti-ideological than it had ever been in the past. Neither an intellectual novelty nor something beyond Marxism in the manner of the innumerable "new departures" launched periodically on the market by intellectual lightweights,[1] this theory is rather the intelligence of the practical conditions necessary *to begin using it*. Thus far Marxism has served just about everyone except proletarians themselves (the work required for neutralizing them is commonly called "Marxism"). The theory that sees its formulation and communication as a single historical task of giving proletarianized real life its autonomous critical language simultaneously returns to it the revolutionary ideas that had been *preserved* separately as ideology, before they were *recuperated* in the course of the prevailing cultural disintegration.

The Situationist International (SI) ushered in a new era by knowing how to draw the old one to a close: ideas are *dangerous* again. In the class war that is beginning again today everywhere, the *situationist moment* is that moment when the proletariat learns to name its modernized misery, discovers the immensity of its task and, within the same movement, becomes reacquainted with its lost history; its *first* victory was the collapse of the counterfeit social unity proclaimed by the spectacle. But already before this moment came to an end, and while its shock wave continued to spread throughout the whole of social life, the SI had to take on board all the consequences of its success, the effects of which it experienced in practice over the checkered course of its latter-day existence.[2] By managing to articulate all the reasons for this failure, and why it had ceased to be effective, the SI truly *began* a new era.

By the time the spectacle was able and obliged to recognize the SI as a recuperated extremism and a political-cultural representation of the real movement, the SI played the nasty trick on it of disappearing. Consequently, the prey had to be wholly consigned to the shadows, whereupon all the crumb-catchers found employment. And while situationist theory encounters those who use it and now discover the need for it in the form of proletarians who reappropriate, verify, and criticize this first formulation of their modern revolutionary necessities by modifying it in the light of experience, whatever remains at the level of culture gets managed by the recuperators as spectacular thinking at the end of the world of the spectacle.

The seriousness of the current social crisis can be seen in the spectacle itself, insofar as the unarmed grandiloquence into which the old revolutionary movement has so often fallen—with its moralizing nonsense about how to improve this society—is today essentially the work of power and its agents. Of all the strikes through which proletarians are beginning to ruin this world, the greatest obstacle remains the one targeting the spectacle's own *pointless phraseology*, evidence already of their anti-ideological consciousness: "for it is forces that easily acquire names, not names forces" (Machiavelli).

§

The submissive thought of the preceding period, which shamelessly pontificated with impunity about everything, held sway only because it ruled under the guarantee of an otherwise effective authority: a society that had temporarily succeeded in silencing its enemies and in organizing the omnipresent spectacle of its victory—the repression of historical memory. Our recuperators today are not in as good a position; yet it is only to the collapse of reconstituted false memories that they owe their employment, after the short-lived antihistoric triumphalism of structuralism, not that the latter is in short supply for the purpose of renewing academic enquiry at a time when the entirety of survival has become *problematic*. But confusionist falsification must now operate in the heat of the moment, faced with active, practical opposition. And once the facts begin to speak for themselves, spectacular explanation arrives too late.

At issue here is obviously not any concern over the intellectual poverty of professionalized thinking, but rather a dispassionate acknowledgment of how refined and *sophisticated* this misery has become in recent history, that is to say, by virtue of the struggles shaping it. No longer does any professor, to the instant acclamation of their entire student body, consider their work complete without the inclusion of a radical critique of knowledge, the latest addition to the new university curriculum. By falsifying the history of culture, the first modernist academics created a counterfeit culture, a corporatist code whose tics serve as certificates for those schooled in modern illiteracy. At the same time, however, artisanship was lost in the transition to the industrial age, as was the craft of falsification itself, which presupposes a minimum of no-nonsense information. And when exhausted, separated thought tries to make the headlong rush into informal decomposition, it manages to come up with nothing better in Portugal than that ridiculous braggart Carvalho, whose extremism captured global headlines, yet whose bizarre brand of council communism lasted only one summer.[3]

Having reached a degree of liquefaction joyfully proclaimed as the pinnacle of thought, the dizzying decline in the quality of cultural products merely expresses the fact that the sector responsible for producing justifications for this unjustifiable society, in ongoing accord with the criteria it itself has laid down, has embarked on a downward spiral to the point where it is no longer even able *to justify itself*. Psychiatrists excusing madness, doctors questioning medical treatments, economists inveighing against commodity relations, journalists lambasting news items, scholars discovering that they are at the service of power, teachers scornful of learning, union leaders fixated on self-management—all are modeled on that improbable Maoist priest Cardonnel, who coolly but theologically denies the existence of God.[4] Although they openly admit that specializations are collapsing, their modesty prompts them to claim that these ruins can still serve as material for a new specialism. Whereas in the past their superior knowledge meant that they had to be trusted, nowadays they are supposed to be trusted because they have scaled back their claims and democratically propose that we all "work together," as they say, that is, under their leadership as specialists in ignorance, new medicine, new economics, new information, etc.

Against the backdrop of the system's collapse, the above flotsam stands in the same relation to separated thought as urbanism does to those interior designers of late US capitalism who are now building mock-ruined supermarkets: "Walls torn to pieces as if by an explosion, a section of collapsed façade releasing a shower of rubble" (*L'Express*, September 1–7, 1975). However, contrary to what this French journalist thinks it safe to say, we are not dealing here with the "illusion of self-destructive architecture" by means of which capitalism could still "enrich itself by feigning its own collapse." Rather, it is now common knowledge that this collapse is only too real, and that the architecture of alienation is quite literally on autodestruct, as can be seen in the decadence of US cities even before they are razed to the ground by proletarians. If there is an illusion somewhere, it is in the prospect of eliminating the real disaster through such means. The French aristocracy of the eighteenth century also enjoyed fake ruins: yet that didn't prevent their castles from being burned to the ground.

This society, which had been dying in the habit of its survival, now seems to survive only by the habit of its death throes. Although the decay of the world of the commodity is familiar, it is not yet known: in the broadest sense, recuperation is the organization of this simultaneous familiarity and ignorance.

§

Recuperators no longer possess an antihistorical force ever since the social organization that employs them lost it. They crudely attempt to compensate for it in a carnivalesque style by proclaiming everything that preceded them obsolete: when it comes to the cultural junk of an earlier period, it is difficult to argue with them. Yet they are not the ones responsible, always so tolerant as they are with their colleagues. Their hype about the virtues of perpetual renewal merely serves the purpose of avoiding to *situate* themselves in relation to the revolutionary thought of history, that of Marx or the SI, which they well know is impenetrable to them and something they would prefer to jettison. Truth be told, the world has not changed much since Marx: for example, the dominant ideas are still essentially the ideas of the dominant class. The fact that there can be a place for such nonsensical chatter as in Lyotardian philosophy, or in the economics à la Jacques Attali, only indicates that this ruling class—under pressure to reorganize its domination as soon as possible with no idea about how to go about it—is now blindly pulling out all the stops of ideological futurism, with the same inability to choose that characterizes every aspect of its management of society.

As for the extent to which this world has changed since Marx, it has become more *profoundly* what it already was; this is precisely what the critical theory of the spectacle was able to grasp. And recuperators, who are perforce wherever this theory is for the purpose of neutralizing it, readily concede that it is Marxist. In their eyes, this is even its principal defect, a regrettable attachment to a past that prevented it from being as modern as it could have been, if only it had been a bit bolder—the type of boldness programmed so well by the shameless Lyotard: "We need not leave the place where we are, we need not be ashamed to speak in a 'state-funded' university."[5] It is indeed true that for a whole generation of tenured intellectuals, petrified Marxism was never anything more than a form of their guilty conscience, incarnated in the Parti Communiste Français (PCF) in the worst cases, or, for the more honest ones, in a grouplet like Socialisme ou Barbarie.[6] Now they want to enjoy their "position" without shame. But since their position is shameful, their enjoyment is a sham, just like the self-justifications they boorishly publicize. Thus, the dizzying novelty that they ceaselessly hype for the purpose of rendering Marx, dialectics, theory, history, and, above all, the proletariat obsolete naturally remains a phantom: like every other modern commodity they want to enjoy "without shame," recuperators are more noisy than useful.

Certainly not all recuperators are as *advanced* as Lyotard in the business of decomposing apologetics. But even if their competitive shirking of responsibility is understated, it is comical to see that the contempt for historical time, so gloriously trumpeted, bars them from making spectacular use as and when required of anything innovative or significant that they themselves have been able to come up with and which is precisely what *qualifies* them as recuperators. Having rallied unconditionally to the dominant falsification of the history of ideas, they can no longer even maintain the truth about the history of their own ideas. Thus, Castoriadis must provide lengthy prefaces explaining that the texts he is unearthing are well and truly superseded by more recent discoveries. He has no great difficulty persuading the reader of the current banality of his former ultra-leftism. Less successful, however, are his attempts to differentiate his later work from the banalities currently all the rage, a distinction he proclaims in punchy adspeak along the lines of "Ober-Pils Draft: draft beer bottled." Then there is Lefort, having loud fun to the faint echo of ideas that he more fully espoused in harsher times,[7] pretending to discover in the flimsy aspirations of the Mouvement du 22 Mars what he had known all along, but better. Or even "Ratgeb" (formerly Raoul Vaneigem), who refrains from sweeping his pet subjects, history and revolution, under the carpet,[8] instead jettisoning all these matters too embarrassed to say anything about the SI and what it accomplished. A craze for pseudonyms among these pseudo-pioneers will therefore come as no surprise, damaged goods who hope to fool people by changing labels. On the other hand, Castoriadis, after a string of pseudonyms, imagines that he has taken a new lease on life by reverting to his real name.

§

The recuperator processes the only raw material this society doesn't deplete but produces in ever increasing quantities: dissatisfaction with its disastrous results. But since the recuperator is himself only a pathetic fragment of these disastrous results, all this material is processed in an unsatisfactory manner. His target audience is therefore composed of exactly those who may pretend to be satisfied with his gimmicks in the same way that they pretend to be satisfied with all the commodities they consume in their capacity as today's managers (*cadres*) who, aping the likes of Lyotard, luxuriate in both submission and refusal, their happiness as false as their refusal and faked just as badly. A recuperator who does the thinking for managers is nevertheless only a thinking manager. Think about it.

Thus, like those marginally privileged managers who, among other unfortunates, sit in the same traffic jams every night to get out of Paris but feign the belief that the hassle nevertheless affords them a semblance of quiet, rural solitude, recuperators are as unconvincing as they are convinced of their loud claims to originality. Finding themselves caught up in the same mounting chaos where a multitude of radical and challenging questions spring up overnight like mushrooms, they all imagine themselves to be venturing out upon their own heroic investigations, unaware that any one of their own colleagues uses the same technique of frantic questioning, always undaunted when it comes to tearing apart the past and the future, but completely silent on their bleak submission to the present. Total saturation of the market does more than anything else, however, to highlight their true condition as hard-up paper-pushers: in short, their books do not sell.

Between worn-out gossip and sensationalism masquerading as news, everyone has to have their own schtick as a brand image according to the same commercial logic that in the art world began hyping painters with easily identifiable styles, such as Modigliani or Utrillo, for idiots who fancy themselves connoisseurs, so that painting itself better conforms to these sales techniques and to painters like Buffet or Mathieu and their ilk.[9] Thus, as the new must be upheld wherever it is found, recuperation proceeds by isolating an aspect of revolutionary criticism that may be crystallized into a new analytic system (Henri Lefebvre pioneered this technique with the critique of urbanism);[10] but even as a fragment shorn of its dialectical relationship to the totality, the recuperator does not know how to use what he recuperates: these people for whom any object must serve as an exercise in publicity naturally end up, through this formal activity, with an inverted content that imposes a stamp of triviality upon the form.

In the market of recuperation, each individual commodity fights for itself and proclaims the inferiority of all others, even allowing the articulation of something true in the process, as frequently occurs when one commodity out-hypes its rivals. The stage is then set for the comical clash of umpteen lesser recuperations, wherein one recuperator handles the imagination while another deals with the libido, each plying their own distinctive gimmick. Elsewhere, if it's not the "dramaturgical society" that dominates us,[11] then surely it must be the "discourse of power,"[12] either that or the burden of ancient Greek thought that Hegel and Marx handed down to us. In one way or another, all these people declaim against the "tyranny of discourse," and denounce the authoritarianism underlying all intellectual activity (cue Ratgeb, who declares theoretical analysis obsolete). Yet thoughtless hucksters remain quite simply *unreadable*.

Clearly highest on this rapidly disintegrating learning curve ("A student could acquire a considerable amount of literary knowledge by saying the opposite of what the poets of this century have said"[13]), those less concerned with saving face coolly demonstrate the superiority of their junk on the grounds that it bears no relation to rational thought. Busy spreading their trash over this dunghill of the glorified unconscious are all the neo-clerics, ranging from Illich to the slimy Clavel via a kind of Mouvement du 22 Mars of religious belief casually preaching out of a cesspit called Taizé.[14]

Descending one floor down to small-time careerism, the revival of various *techniques* developed by revolutionary critique is worthy of note, used here as hollow procedures and fashionable mannerisms: *détournement* in order to mine a bit more from the age-old literary seam, as practiced by Maoist scumbags like Sollers;[15] the insipid popularization of dated "underground comix" antics;[16] subtitled films à la René Viènet (subtitling is not *détournement*);[17] or the soap opera staging of certain nonconformist *attitudes* in serial literary production, from Manchette to Guégan.

§

There is stiff competition for a position in the market of recuperation. However, not everyone has a past to negotiate, one subject to rapid wear and tear in these inflationary times swollen by the ever-renewed influx of apprentice recuperators attracted by the little skill required. This new generation, whose lamentable beginnings we are now witnessing, embarks on their careers at the same time that their elders are still pursuing theirs— although, as we have seen, this hardly constitutes an insurmountable obstacle, since extremist one-upmanship does not require great intellectual resources. Any rookie who has never been anywhere will nevertheless swear that he is well and truly back: great revolutionary illusions were all well and good when he was young and enthusiastic circa 1969. Now he looks to the future, determined to maximize forthwith the small bit of politico-cultural capital he acquired during those glory days as a youth, but which is currently at serious risk of collapse. By now he considers it accomplishment enough to have remained proudly stuck, year in and year out, in his revolutionist pose and to have eked out a living well away from the places he thinks he is in urgent demand, in publishing or elsewhere. The hour of rewards has come: in short, he wants success, and fast. But as so many others have pored over and used the same books as he has, he must stand out from the crowd, something he is totally incapable of doing. He will therefore get stuck in some ongoing scam, either that or, displaying a thin veneer of erudition, resort to a Marxological purism ensuring his access—now that Rubel is flagging—to some subaltern job in publishing.[18] And if Bordigism is not your thing,[19] then there's always the Frankfurt School.

More than anywhere else, it is among this new wave of recuperators that recuperation will be excoriated with all the rancor of an audience at a film screening who see that some craze they themselves kicked off has now spread everywhere. As incapable as any union bureaucrat of understanding that confusionist recuperation is the product of a real, albeit still chaotic, movement to whose reality they have remained consistently oblivious but on whose future and fate of its struggle the meaning of widely discredited words ultimately depends, recuperators have merely settled for wild speculation about its invincibility, either instantly in the form of total revolution lifting them out of their mediocrity, or along more conventional lines in the form of some prestigious role garnering limitless kudos from society together with sufficient cash grants to keep them going.

The theorizing enthusiasm of recuperators usually begins with the obvious fact that the SI was of its time, which is now over, and then reaches a peak with the discovery that they themselves must therefore be better, indeed their arrival in the wake of the SI historically guarantees their great and unique superiority. In order to break the good news, they will take the opportunity to preface another writer's work, a pretext to sneak in a few of their own little ideas since they are incapable of writing the book they always imagined they would. Not being full-fledged authors, they easily find employment in scholarly packaging—not that they are scholars, but since every publisher eager to tap into the new revolutionary book market is generally so ignorant of these matters, they have no option but to leave it to those offering their services. But what can people with no future say about the past, let alone the present? The fact is they are not really interested in the past except as an opportunity to deposit their quasi-cultish ideas and, strewn over dead bodies, settle a few outstanding questions in a spirit of infallible scientific prognostication: they must at least give their opinion on the history of class struggle from its origins to the present day, the means and goals of communist revolution, and the true nature of modern capitalism. If they talk about what they preface, it is in order to belittle it—their way of saying that the work is menial in nature and far beneath them. The prize in this respect must go to the stupefying Guégan who, back when he was still trying his hand at theory, regaled the reader of Georges Darien with absurd "theses" on the latter amounting to a conclusion of three lines of biographical material preceded by a haughty "for that's him in the last analysis."[20]

The limited fund of knowledge displayed by these neophytes is certainly very out of date, but it should be acknowledged that what they conceal is hardly more original, the form thus in perfect accord with the content. Indeed, there is nothing new about the existence of a sub-intelligentsia employed in junior positions for the upkeep and distribution of cultural values produced by others. But today the *abandonment* of creation and free thinking, which are finding fuller employment ranged against this society and its culture, together with the large-scale creation of jobs devoted to managing and concealing this void, means that this mob of arrogant ignoramuses now find themselves able to inherit the management of all the crumbling old specializations, the most bullish among them imagining that they can arrive there even faster via today's specialized shortcut: by representing critical thinking. In the absence of any criterion of value, all they have to do to stand out from the crowd is to put something new on the market. They are nevertheless impoverished in this respect, having been educated and trained according to standards of approbation and conformism.

§

Over the last seven years more ideas have been developed among recuperators than would be needed to save the old world, if these ideas could only form an ideology of some kind of development; but for that to happen, it would still be necessary to ideologize the real revolutionary movement and furnish it with misconceptions and partial goals that blind it to the totality of its significance and its project. Our recuperators are in no way up to the task, able only to affirm the impossibility and futility of social revolution, while the masses, inconveniently exploited enough to desire such a revolution, would be better off by quickly adhering to idiotic *gimmicks* (struggling to get it up, that repugnant Lyotard goes so far as to write that "the insane plea of the masses" is not "Long Live the Social Revolution" but "Long live the Libidinal Economy!"[21]). As for being a fan, like Ratgeb, of the immediate possibility of revolution and the grotesque trappings of a self-managed obstacle course that he lends it, exactly the same wholesale detachment from reality applies.

In fact, this is in no way a process of ideological alienation organically linked to the development of revolutionary struggle as its false consciousness, but a matter of bits and pieces of ideology conjoined with the disintegration of values in the spectacle, since this is the sphere where its bearers find employment without having to put their careers as ideologues on hold pursuant to any change in existing conditions. For revolutionary ideas to exist, there must be a revolutionary class. But the modern revolutionary class, the proletariat, has no revolutionary ideas of its own apart from the consciousness of its action: until such time as the proletariat takes back these ideas by resuming their struggle, they lead an independent existence within the sphere of culture; that is to say, appropriated or, more to the point, *exploited* like the proletariat itself by specialized intellectuals. The condition of these intellectuals in society determines their use of revolutionary ideas and their illusions about that use. Under different historical conditions, this can yield either Bolshevism or recuperators in spectacular culture: let's say the case is all a matter of *careerist discharge*. Today these cultural workers, who in other times would have been social democrats or Bolsheviks, no longer need revolutionary illusions, and thus the most cynical among them naturally end up proclaiming that the need for revolution is merely an illusion.

Even more than for traditional far-left debris propelled back into action by the visible return of the social revolution in May 1968 at a time when this very same flotsam was mellowing out in universities or in the psychoanalytic field, the spineless submission to the miserable conditions of employment afforded these low-skilled, non-manual workers, mass produced by the current education system, is attributable to the absence of an employer who might better satisfy their corporatist ambitions and extremist illusions; that is to say, a hierarchical party complete with a revolutionary ideology under their control. What remains of leftist sects can satisfy only the most narrow-minded, who often, after sowing their wild oats in activist posturing, quietly join the PCF, which can at least offer them the chance to participate straightaway in the management of this society, many of whose cultural sectors it already outsources. But for those who are nevertheless more demanding and modern, and whose aspirations are less realistic when it comes to revolutionary illusions, they need nothing less than the management of *mass situationism* to direct their satisfaction. Yet they were never satisfied. Some even went to considerable lengths themselves to organize a councilist-inflected version of it but soon became discouraged. High-end consumers of revolutionary images have therefore been busy at work, with many of them landing jobs for the express purpose of organizing and expanding this consumption. As for the production side of things, they have greater problems, as we have seen.

All the asinine opponents and defenders of Marxism, endlessly quibbling over a thousand uninteresting details, say nothing about the only critical truth pertaining to this whole issue which is far too close for comfort to their own social function: the alienated labor movement, and to the highest degree German Social Democracy, had reproduced and bureaucratically instituted the existing division of labor within the ruling class, between those ideologues who elaborate the illusion that this class entertains about itself and those who are its active members but understand their own action only through these ideas and illusions. The recuperation of Marxism, the model of all recuperation to come, has no other basis than this surrender to intellectuals of the task of expressing proletarian points of view, and therefore of expressing them *scientifically* in the dominant language of society, the errors or weaknesses in Marx's theory being of entirely secondary importance in light of this separation from the practical milieu *where they could be corrected*.

Recuperation can deal only partially with what ideological preservation has already *made frigid*. In a world where the spectacle has realized the artistic representation of lived experience and the political representation

of social life in the same monopoly of unilateral exposition, revolutionary theory had to learn each time to
calculate its ever shifting relation to the negative forces
whose program it formulates, never to become their
on-screen representation but to remain *molten* in the
process of its encounter with the practice seeking it out
and never to serve as a basis for any scientific authority whatsoever. (Lautréamont's observation that "in the
new science, each thing comes in its turn, such is its
excellence" is the most apposite in this respect.) The fact
is that this theory is produced by determined individuals, individuals who have achieved self-determination
in the course of practical struggle among the irreconcilable enemies of the spectacle and by acknowledging
their own absence wherever the latter are absent. And
thus we have a clearer picture of the predicament faced
by these intellectual beasts of burden who would prefer
to rattle on about their misery and quiz each other about
solutions, when all they had to do was not go there in
the first place.

Thus, recuperation is not an intellectual problem
that could be solved by means of dogmatic redefinition
of critical concepts; even less is it literary, referring to
some abstract demand for permanent linguistic inno-
vation (cf. the failure of surrealism). It is rather an eminently practical question inseparable from the task of
today's revolutionaries to organize autonomous proletarian communication.

§

In light of the foregoing considerations, it must be concluded that the modern recuperator merely fulminates within an insoluble contradiction: busy planning a future for a spectacular thought entirely conditioned by its inability and unwillingness to grasp its own material basis in the spectacular system, the recuperator must at the same time account both for this system's collapse and for the historical movement responsible for its dissolution. Thus, the recuperator can say nothing about what he recuperates, yet cannot talk about anything else. This is why the recuperator stutters. From the overt irrationalism of academic neo-philosophy to the fantasies of the impossible rationalization of ecological neo-economics, the same anodyne noise can be heard that rings only in the ears of those making it. What was never rational has simply lost the means of appearing so.

The recuperator formulates the self-management of alienation as a *program*, either individually (Attali, Parti Socialiste [PS]/Conféderation Française Démocratique du Travail [CFDT intellectuals, etc.) or socially (Lyotard and those droning on about desire). Yet this only expresses *nostalgia* for an integration that has already failed: the initiative of workers keeping the system running against its own rules, or the pursuit of pleasure in spectacular consumption. This program is now the self-conscious essence of this day and age, the last argument that current society can set against it, its revolutionary transformation and the quintessence of the theoretical output of the prevailing illiteracy. The fact that what was self-evident in terms of a daily compromise with what exists needs to be demonstrated and proposed in this way, as a goal to be achieved, speaks volumes, however, about the loss of control by the powers that be over real proletarianized life.

The false alarmism of apocalyptic merchants attempts to conjure up an impending disaster via the image of a familiar one (economic crisis) or a completely surreal one (ecological catastrophe), thus enabling the spectacle to hark back nostalgically to its eco-fascist youth, for which its entire media sets the stage. As commodity abundance collapses, the organic composition of the illusion must be modified: less material and more ideology. Outside Portugal too, "it is no longer Stalinism that is decomposing, but society, which, by decomposing, becomes Stalinist."[22] Thus, like "eco-nationalism," there could be, if required, a Stalinism without Stalinists. But all this is still just a bureaucratic pipe dream lacking any means for its realization.

As a general rule, when the reality of state power slips away, it is a dangerous game to try to keep up appearances. The external appearance of strength can sometimes bolster a weak body, but more often than not, it finishes it off. Modern states are particularly prone to fall into this error since the power of appearances has long been sufficient to guarantee social peace and stability. Absolutely corrupted by their experience of contempt for reality and the fleeting success of this contempt, they believe they can avoid the rope by denying the existence of hemp.

But as far as hemp is concerned, we know that low-level drug dealers are themselves habitual addicts, unlike those who stand to make a substantial profit. The same holds true for our little dealers in spectacular drugs: professional degeneration hits the degenerating professional harder than anything else (so much for the academic question of their subjective and personal illusions). While undoubtedly among specialists in repression there are people lucid enough about the gravity of the current social crisis, the employees of spectacular culture and information entertain more illusions than anyone else about their own expertise in bluffing and find comfort in the images of reformist planning and euphoric novelties that they themselves serially produce. The increasingly entrenched habits of their profession, the result of their enjoyment of a long-undisputed monopoly, have rendered them little able to determine what is real and true. Thus, those lulling people to sleep have themselves fallen asleep, much like the cameraman in Chile who, clearly not privy to the fact that the image might have other than cinematic consequences for this own life, filmed a soldier taking aim and shooting him.

The activity of recuperators falls entirely within this framework of the mechanical continuation of spectacular monologue having the same contempt for reality that believes it can talk about anything with no thought to the consequences, since it has acquired the right to speak in the existing organization of culture and has never been bothered about consequences. As for the future freeloading prospects of the likes of Ratgeb through to Attali, their two-bit hucksterisms are difficult to distinguish: the former plans an *ongoing* revolution for which he cannot find words and of which he can no longer even *approve*, while the latter makes plans for a future counterrevolution on which he has no idea where to start and cannot even *name*.

Recuperation cheapens revolutionary ideas, but it cheapens them as separate ideas; it ages them prematurely while pitting them against its half-baked claims to usher in the new. Yet what remains young in this world grown old is the project of their coherent and practical use, whose necessity is, *on the contrary*, thrown into sharper relief by recuperated contortions.

Even the word "communism" still has its full meaning *before it*: the coming revolutions will be able to wrest it from the Stalinists, just as the Portuguese revolution has already begun to do.

Small Dictionary of the Great Names of Recuperation

Author's Note

While there's still time, I am prompted to do a head count of the great names of recuperation. Although equally deserving, not all of them are famous; perhaps the most fitting homage to them is to group their names together and scupper their glory. Our era is so ungrateful! It quietly relishes what is done on its behalf and often ignores its benefactors. We must therefore force it to sit up and take notice by painting a portrait of our heroes of recuperation, and by outlining their personalities and achievements for its edification. I shall endeavor to execute the task with all the patience that such an undertaking demands, bearing in mind that the subject matter is so vast that the treatment accorded it here can in no way claim to be exhaustive. It will rather consist of a collection of specimens where I am at least given to think that none of the main species currently known to science has escaped my scrutiny, leaving only the classification of the subspecies, hybrids, and various aberrations to the many scientific vocations that this pioneering work is sure to launch. And if, for the sake of the reader, I have been obliged to choose from so many leading intellectual grovelers, those not named herein will owe me no less gratitude, and awareness of their merits will help them, in no small way, to overcome such an omission.

This dictionary hereby considers the following in turn: a thinker of the state (Attali, the Scourge of the Spectacle), ultra-leftist debris (Castoriadis, the Land-of-Make-Believe-Dupe), a squidgy structuralist (Foucault, the Tenured-Anti-Law-and-Order-Sucker), university dust (Franklin, the Non-Teaching-Philosophy-Casualty),[1] a deliquescent leftist (Glucksmann, the Anti-Marxism-Square), an unexceptional mover and shaker (Guégan, the Child-of-Godard-and-fizzy-Chablis), a professor of decomposition (Lyotard, the Voluptuary-of-the-Positive), and finally, a superannuated Vaneigemist (Ratgeb, the Council-Communism-Spouting-Dried-Up-Piece-of-Toast).

We never read a dictionary cover to cover. The alphabetical ordering deters us from it. Thus, readers bent on absorbing this gallery in one breath will soon come to grief, the accumulation of entries conveying a tedious impression of diversity totally devoid of any content. Yet this is precisely what these commentaries all have in common. At least I am conscious of the fact that brevity is today the most prized form of respect among the general public.

Attali, Jacques

In his successive books (*L'anti-économique*, coauthored with Marc Guillaume, but above all *La parole et l'outil*) —as well as in the countless interviews, colloquia, talks, and roundtables where he has been busily putting his multifaceted idiocy on display—Attali has established himself without a shadow of a doubt as a paragon of the kind of flashy pseudo-science that, in today's France, works its way to the forefront everywhere, trying to cover up the silence of its demise with the roar of its turbo-charged junk. An elite student originally set to study economics but placed for his sins on the open market at a time when this technique of the regulation and control of capitalist domination is finding its means largely unequal to the task, Attali had the gumption to retrain and the ambition to put his mind to retraining other trash like him. As a badge of his modernity, he loftily proclaims the collapse of economics, a discipline he nevertheless continues to teach, even setting his sights specifically and with a further nod to modernity on the *qualitative* collapse of the world whose growth was measured and regulated by political economy. Here he is even more modern, since, while talking about the impotence of leaders, the end of capitalism, and a number of other grievances shared by economist flunkeys, his clumsiness stops short of simply presenting the hardly credible Mitterrandism as the solution to all these ills, despite the fact that he himself is one of its chief strategists. He has bigger fish to fry: *"Awareness of the physical limits of commodity production must lead to the discovery of other limitless horizons fostering the creativity of all human beings."*[2]

"The most precious capital, the most decisive capital, is the human being"[3] thus stands revealed as the core of Attali's agenda, seeing it as his mission to manage its value, although he's not the only one. At a time when the commodity economy must falsify every single aspect of its shattered landscape and acknowledge that it has in no way enriched the powers of humanity or done much, for that matter, about the ruin of the earth not just beneath our feet, it is still, via the terrorism of scarcity, attempting to retrieve the support it once obtained through the terrorism of abundance and has now irretrievably lost. Not every leader, however, is wracked by a sudden concern for "the creativity of all human beings." But, called upon to kickstart the creative surge, now is the time: Attali promises us as much with the bonanza of a few limitless horizons.

In short, all the false needs mass-produced by the dictatorship of the economy are now concentrated in the false need of the economy itself, which is no longer self-evident and must therefore be imposed. Hence the need, according to Attali, for "a political project that is more exciting than the one referred to by most of the economic theories of the past two centuries,"[4] after he has boldly noted "that if the commodity system serves capital [but what else could it serve?], it becomes an obstacle to development."[5]

As for arousing the enthusiasm of the masses, this apostle of a commodity system without capital stands no chance: when he tries his hand at utopia, he is more a sad, encumbered Cabet than a sad, castrated Fourier.[6] He shamelessly raves about the foretaste of those future joys of a free society that, in his view, consist of car radios and pseudo-games in which this society allows people to indulge and participate. After such a Dionysian beginning, the monumental upheaval he advocates is nevertheless tempered by the news that the state, no more than the commodity, will not be abolished so easily (this is where Mitterrand shows the cloven hoof). And when he acts the visionary, he writes that the man of the future, if everything goes according to Attali's plan, will be "highly knowledgeable, linked to memory machines, performing semantic cybernetic operations on man's behalf."[7] Meanwhile, Attali will be grazing on punch cards. But for the time being, the IBM mainframe he plugged himself into to write his latest book must have crashed, undoubtedly depressed by the ridiculous appearance of its human appendage, since its information is curiously flawed and its memory failing.

Attali throws topics around like confetti: "communication, such a vague word and a poorly understood problem"; "the analysis of connectivity remains today the almost absolute, perhaps insoluble, methodological mystery"[8] (this imbecile has rebranded *dialogue* as "connectivity"); "little is known about inequality";[9] etc. But his attempts here to cover up his limited creativity with a few limitless horizons are ultimately pointless, since the unevenness of the sources he uses to supply his intellectual poverty is only too plain. There is no doubt that he pads out his writing with one perfectly clichéd trope after the other, namely with puns worthy of Lacan's almanac, inept neologisms in the style of Barthes, biology à la Morin,[10] while among those he quotes is just about anyone who writes any old nonsense (he has thus learned from Lyotard that "man is the work of his works": poor Lyotard! Poor Attali!). But once his prose has been stripped of all this dismal clutter on loan, what could be left but an even greater quantity of journalistic platitudes on top of what was already there, peppered with scientific vulgarization and accompanied by graphics and diagrams? After one hundred and fourteen pages of this lamentable suspense, Attali finally plays his high card in the form of his social prophecy: "but moreover, a third era in the explosive process is now beginning"[11]—I have spared the reader the first two, and as for the "explosive process," it is simply capitalist development—"an era whose megatools are not material but information-based, where man is repressed without violence, an era of the *passive repression* of relationships, of the *society of the spectacle*."[12] It was time for him to take ideas wherever they could be found, since he still had half of a book to finish.

We have thus discovered the theoretical talisman of this Attila the Hun of economic thought, a lucky charm that provides the impetus for him to embark on something for which he is so obviously unsuited: here we have a junior state official, a professor at the École Polytechnique, and an advisor to Mitterrand who has read *The Society of the Spectacle*. As quite a rare species, he assumes that this is enough to qualify him as a thinker, and even as a leader, coolly presenting his *arriviste* credentials in the following terms: "In fact, almost everywhere, economic and political responsibilities are exercised by men who, if they ever studied economics, did so thirty years ago, in books written at least forty years ago."[13] Attali is a Situationist in the very specific sense laid down by the Larousse dictionary:[14] he is "against the social situation that favors the current generation."[15]

The whole second half of Attali's book is thus nothing more than his own concoction of thinly disguised waffle: he talks at length about "dramaturgical society," "interpersonal initiatives," self-management and "implosive processes," only to end by declaring, with all the cynicism of a recuperator victimized by recuperation, that he is aware that all of these wonderful discoveries could be distorted by "the champions of an extreme form of the society of the spectacle into a worldwide *panem et circenses* with less bread and more spectacle."[16] Watch out, Attali: playing games might make you short-circuit and implode.

In the course of nonstop mentions of all sorts of unusable books, nowhere does he mention the only book he does use. However, while the title of *The Society of the Spectacle* is mentioned, neither its content nor author is: a superfluous epigraph to one of Attali's chapters informs the reader that "the spectacle is capital to such a degree of accumulation that it becomes mirage."[17] So capital has become a mirage, and Attali himself is doubtless just a potted plant in the lobby of the state council—either that or École Polytechnique got a lot more than it bargained for. This surprising visual discovery is attributed by Attali to an uncertain "Guy Debré" in his book *The Society of the Spectacle*, which must have been published secretly under such a pseudonym. With a sudden eye for forensic detail, Attali nevertheless sees fit to give the exact *page reference* where this particular brainchild is to be found, but which is merely a mirage in the middle of the desert of his worthlessness, no doubt born of the refraction of an idea in the tepid miasmas of his brain.

This, then, is how Attali resolves the contradiction of the recuperator who knows that, just as some people use others as mere stepping-stones, his plagiarism may serve only to bring what he recuperates to the attention of those as yet unversed in it. The kind of typographical modification ("mirage" for "image") that goes to the heart of Attalian orthographic and modernist antics (e.g., "the new e-era [*l'erre nouvelle*]," "the sign field [*le champ du signe*]"[18]) casts an even brighter light on what he meant in his previous work by "the study of human beings in their social totality, in their temporal continuity, in their everyday life (following in Henri Lefebvre's footsteps),"[19] to which he added "is one for which all techniques are useful." He is at any rate hot on the heels of Lefebvre when it comes to a certain temporal continuity of falsification by matching him in the only technique in which the latter really excelled, that of the *prefabricated typo*[20] with the kind of scientific integrity that consists in balancing a volume of painstaking plagiarism with a bit of butchered quotation,[21] accompanied by some mangled reference whose page number is nevertheless correct.

Thus, Attali's intellectual method is not terribly new and he himself is not up to the job, unlike his imitator Marc Guillaume who is now busy independently recuperating the latest refinement brought into this area by a wave of post-Lefebvrist charlatans demonstrating what could be construed as a plausible awareness of the SI and its theses.[22] Their reference to the SI is only a minor point of no importance, a triviality suggesting that the rest of what the SI has to say is even less interesting (or of recently endorsing the critique of the spectacle via gross distortion: the Oscar for slanderous praise going to the incorrigible returnee Régis Debray, who extols *The Society of the Spectacle* for having foreseen the 1974 electoral defeat of the French left as far back as 1967).[23] Chief too among the charlatans is the neo-Bordigist Barrot, who, in his cumbersome Marxish compilation entitled *Eclipse and Re-Emergence of the Communist Movement*,[24] indicates in a footnote that the SI was, "among other things" (that remain unmentioned), one of the best expressions of this refusal of militantism and of what it represents and conceals;[25] yet this refusal of militantism was not some eureka moment conjured up by the SI but a crucial feature of contemporary history, something that must have come to Barrot's own attention in the grouplets where he had been vegetating away. And inasmuch as it touches upon everything else, what has the SI achieved by turning this refusal into a positive project? On the evidence given here, there is a good chance that Barrot's heavily circumscribed readership will not be finding out anytime soon. Having moved to Paris and fresh-mouthing his times in the form of an afterword for a grotesque book series entitled "Critique of Politics" (whose red covers are revolutionary in the sense of a pressure cooker adspeak: "What's red and goes fast? Seb pressure cookers!"[26]) is the vile Jean-Yves Bériou, venturing to mention the SI in the same breath as "Socialisme ou Barbarie" among those groups who "emerge fully from a period of counter-revolution," and going on to assert that they "are its most faithful, albeit ambiguous, expression since they peddle all the ideology, all the modernism and false problems linked to the counter-revolution, yet *put their finger firmly* on the new conditions of the coming revolution and go so far as to elaborate a savage critique of all extant theory from a cutting-edge revolution-friendly counterrevolutionary point of view."[27] In the tortuous course of this half-cop, half-raisin verdict, only a single gripe emerges unequivocally in the form of unreconstructed hatred ("the period of revolutionary resumption is occupied by people of different origins")[28] for those who "go so far as" to put not only their finger but their whole hand firmly on slanderers (cf. *SI* issue no. 12, p. 101).[29] Many others could be instanced, including Franklin (see below, were it possible to sink any lower). But the prize still goes to a certain Émile Marenssin—pseudonym of Jacques Baynac, an above average undertaker who did not wait until the members of the ill-starred "Baader-Meinhof Gang" had cooled down before giving, on the occasion of the publication of their hollow Marxist-Leninist proclamations, his opinion on the best way to pass *"from prehistory to history."*[30] In yet another of his prefaces, after giving weighty consideration to the revolutionary merits of *Charlie-Hebdo* or the CFDT, lending ideas to André Glucksmann, and discovering in pop music a "revolutionary breakthrough in the domain of art," he informs us in yet another of his footnotes that "the concept of spectacle reports, but is not operative." Harsh words indeed from such an operative theorist whose "working hypothesis" on the formation of armed organizations has carefully drawn our attention to the fact that "it would be

pointless at present to embark on its practical verifica-
tion." But operative for what? For carving out your own
niche in publishing by prefacing or adding afterwords to
the works of present or past activists? It is understandable that after making a name for himself in this way, he
felt the time was right to change it: Baynac, now under
his real name, sticks his afterword oar into the French
translation of *Out of the Night*, the latest misfortune to
befall Jan Valtin,[31] casually adding, "I'm today having
this eye-witness account republished." Here we find the
stupidity of stooges who want to pass themselves off as
bosses. Attali, on the other hand, enjoying more power
than a hack like Baynac, indulges in the democratic and
paternalistic luxury of including "all those who had a
hand in the manufacture of this book: secretaries, print-
ers, font calibrators" in his acknowledgments,[32] whereas
that other sad hack would have everyone believe that
he decides everything. This is how *spectacular* our recuperators are in every detail: the one who has no power
pretends to have it, while the one who has it pretends to
share it. Now that's operativity for you!

Attali is remarkable only insofar as he is not a vulgar
product of that neo-university which trains junior tech-
nicians in spectacular confusionism, those who only
have the power to make noise. Instead, he has followed
the path by which the French bourgeoisie select those
senior civil servants and managers, those who exercise
real power in the state or at the head of large companies.

His works can therefore be seen as a program for the most modern among these leaders, formulating their tasks and the means to carry them out. Encouraging is not too strong a word for it. Attali is undoubtedly better informed than others, but he uses his information only in a superficial and flashy manner for the purpose of basking in all the appearances of innovative thinking. He clearly does not even believe in his own woolly proposals and, rather than implementing them, is more interested in monetizing them: he rushes in without conviction. (This is the case across the board: a sentence attributed to Breton turns out in fact to be a butchered one from Louis Aragon's *Treatise on Style*; as for Lukács, Attali calls him "Lukas" and simply lifts a quotation of *History and Class Consciousness* from the epigraph of chapter 2 of *The Society of the Spectacle*, a book clearly of great use to him.)

It is not just that all the means are lacking to implement the threadbare proposals for bureaucratic and ecological rationalization, which now flourish by the dozens. It is rather that their formulation is already fundamentally vitiated by the principles of social illusion, since these proposals are themselves nothing but shortsighted expedients that painstakingly rearrange the map while the territory collapses. The fact that the bluster of a technocratic "final solution," which was never anything but the bourgeoisie dreaming of ridding itself of the proletariat, has managed to resurface all jazzed up, sporting an ecological gloss and charged up with computers, is certainly not because it has acquired a greater degree of feasibility: it has in fact already been eliminated by the reign of passivity to which this bluster attached the highest cybernetic importance. It represents merely the latest in a series of scaremongering ploys by that ludicrous international lobby of top executives, ideologues of their déclassé illusory existence who are thus fighting redundancy at a time when states are determined to reduce incidental expenditure in order to focus on *real* repression, not on their own modernist and moralizing trappings.

As unreal in their optimism as in their pessimism, all the chattering prognostications under discussion here have as their extrascientific and unmentionable premise the zeroing out of the unknown variable of their calculations: the proletariat. But those to be wiped out as proletarians are the same ones to be exploited as workers. An old problem to which Stalinism, as we know, is the old answer. Stalinism is the profane reality of what ecology is merely the sacred eloquence. Stalinists, who despise nitpicking, know this only too well: their work is the organization of the absence of the proletariat; workers' alienation is their property.

The torrent of reformist deliberations generated by the crisis of commodity abundance has only one effect on its object, and that is to exacerbate paper shortages, causing this sector of production to work, like all the others, toward its own abolition. Attali's superiority over whatever futurological jingles are out there making the rounds is that both he and his Mitterrandism bank on the bureaucratic forces that already ensure the maintenance of this social organization. There is not a word from him, however, about any of this: like all good recuperators, he cannot do what he talks about, and cannot talk about what he does.

Castoriadis, Cornelius

Ten years after the dissolution of the organization and journal *Socialisme ou Barbarie* into spineless eclecticism (see *I.S.* no. 10, "Socialisme ou Planète"),[33] Castoriadis remains an enemy of history, dialectics, and Marxism, leaving him none of the peace for which he might have been hoping. Our unfortunate times have nevertheless seen to it that the paperback republication of articles for this *Marxist* journal, up to and including its principal thinker's final mutation, provides him with a platform for venting his *anti*-Marxist fury. Delineated here in full is the irony of history and its dialectic, since if his intellectual capitulation and deference to the worst sociological clichés were as promising as he believed they were in his capacity as a fully paid-up member of the Edgar Morin school of confusionism, *Socialisme ou Barbarie* would now rank as a long-forgotten curio and he would in no way require all the publicity hype around its disinterment in order to deposit his latest hunches. But hunches are what currently litter the terrain, and the tragedy of Castoriadis is that his past remains *even newer* than his intellectual present. He had barely settled into a comfortable niche within society following long years worn out by appearances countering him and by his failure to counter appearances when, suddenly, all the pseudo developments he had been raving about were superseded by the real movement whose practical and conscious possibilities he gleefully rejected outright. Indeed, the real movement he thought he was rid of is now responsible, among other things, for the readership of revolutionary Marxist analyses of the past, and for publishers to publish them.

Here, then, is Castoriadis grappling with the ghost of his own thought, which arrives to pull him out of his cozy Freudian sleep, as he comically struggles in his prefaces to sabotage anything of any real importance that the rest of any volume of his might have to say. He even adds grist to the inarticulate investigation, as if the republication of his complete works did not already paint a suitably deplorable picture of his journey to an intellectual cul-de-sac by simply juxtaposing some texts. It is nevertheless true that he chooses not to publish them in chronological order, an order that would at least give *some sense and direction* to anyone not fond of quiet senility.

"That which has perpetuated itself for ten centuries as Rome does not possess a name in any language—and, indeed, could hardly have one,"[34] writes this histrionic thinker, who, elsewhere in his inimitable and stammering flights of fancy, accuses Marx of metaphysical thinking. That non-existence which has perpetuated itself for twenty years as Castoriadis possesses a name in every language—and indeed could hardly have any other.

Wherever revolutionary theory *makes distinctions* by naming them, recuperation works to erase them, to rank them as of only secondary importance, and to dismiss others. The originality of Castoriadis lies in carrying out this work upon his own earlier works. In the first place it is obviously the division of society into classes that now seems outdated to him, as any sociologist would agree: "The working class, in the proper sense of the term, has increasingly tended to become a minority in modern capitalist countries. And, what is even more important, it no longer manifests itself or *claims to be* a class. To be sure, almost all of those who work are now wage labor-ers. What this means, in effect, is that it no longer makes much sense to speak in terms of class."[35] So much for the level and depth of his analysis. But where Castoriadis brilliantly demonstrates his superiority over vulgar so-ciology is that, whereas the common or garden-variety sociologist flatly states that he *cannot see* the proletariat through the fog of his questionnaires and statistics, Cas-toriadis proudly asserts that he does not see the prole-tariat *because he does not want to*. This would in fact put him in the same boat as Marx, "bound to Hegel, Aristotle and Plato."[36] No one, of course, likes to be in bondage, even to such reputable people whose authoritarianism must nonetheless have been adversely affected over the passage of time. In relation to the past, at any rate, Cas-toriadis is determined, however, to maintain his inde-pendence. Yet he is not a master, and we have seen that he has not exactly done himself any favors either: if he is no good to anyone, this is simply because he himself is good for nothing. Should he ever slip up and actually try theorizing, then Castoriadis, anxious to persist in his irrepressible uselessness, would have to think twice about undermining proletarian autonomy, which of course has faced others worse than him. Save me from myself! He is in fact quite the model of self-restraint, and stumbles merrily along over one hundred and twenty pages that this preface takes to steer clear of the question of "the history of the workers' movement" comprising its title. For, as Hegel rightly wrote, "what calls itself fear of error reveals itself rather as fear of the truth."[37]

Our scrupulous defender of the ineffable proletariat gets particularly indignant over Marx's famous assertion that "it is not a question of what this or that proletarian, or even the whole proletariat, at the moment *regards* as its aim. It is a question of *what the proletariat is*, and what, in accordance with this *being*, it will historically be compelled to do" (*The Holy Family*).[38] Castoriadis sees this as an especially pernicious embodiment of "the axiom of the sovereignty of the theoretico-speculative, which underlies all of Western history."[39] From where, then, does Marx get his consciousness of what the proletariat will be historically compelled to do? Presumably from Plato, since, despite his elucubrations, Castoriadis turns out not to have a single clue. "*Where* is this 'being' of the proletariat which will compel it to do what it historically must? Only in Marx's head!"[40] This is a thesis that surely goes beyond every known conspiracy theory up to now concerning the diabolical schemes of the "Red Terror Doctor."[41] Thus, the revolution of 1848, which the proletariat was compelled to forge, must have sprung fully armed from the brain of Marx. And since no revolution, armed or not, has ever sprung from the brain of Castoriadis, we must conclude that Marx is a particularly nefarious "philosopher king" whose posterity is "quite naturally" to be found to in the "great leader of revolutionary science": Stalin.[42]

There is little chance that laughter about Castoriadis's compendious worthlessness will ever be in short supply, although it should be pointed out that this uselessness is shot through with a baseness of a less entertaining nature than this Byzantine Greek nonsense. Already a masterpiece is his use of "quite naturally," referring to the transition from Marx to Stalin with its dismissal of half a century of class struggle and the crushing of the old revolutionary movement. From his antitheoretical heaven, Castoriadis sees only one "being" from Plato to Stalin that, regardless of its purpose, is antihistorically compelled to keep us "in thrall" to the "theoretical and speculative nexus."[43] But then Castoriadis comes along: "It is not easy to break with an attitude that—much more than opinions, external influences and particular socio-historical situations—is rooted in what we have *regarded* for over three thousand years as being, knowledge, and truth—and ultimately in the almost unbeatable necessity for thought itself. I should add that I am speaking from experience."[44] And if needs must, let's all mutate together! For more than ten years now, Castoriadis has been trying to emancipate himself from thought and its "almost unbeatable necessity." The reason he has never advanced one single inch is because he has always been *beside himself.* "Over three thousand years" would be nowhere near long enough to emancipate him from his "bondage," for the yoke under which he is visibly groaning is as heavy as his own gormlessness. And besides, the lordship and bondage dialectic cannot play out in his favor: he is far too unproductive.

Beating a path toward nonthinking, this thinker need not fear falling prey to the insidious evil of dialectical theory since his hidebound positivism gives him total immunity. After conceding that the proletariat "can and does struggle against its exploitation and oppression," he notes that "there is no necessary and *a priori* reason why this struggle should have acquired the dimensions, potency, and content that it did."[45] When it comes to the necessity for thought, now at least he knows all he needs to know concerning necessitarianism. Heaven forbid, though, that he should keep all this to himself: fortuitousness for all and Castoriadis knoweth them that are his![46]

For the proletariat, the continuation of its history is on par with its *a priori* lack of necessity. "Called upon to effect the most radical overturning ever undertaken—the passage from 'prehistory' to real 'history'"[47] for over a century, this class has been, Castoriadis remarks caustically, "prey to tenacious illusions . . . demonstrating an astonishing capacity to believe in deceitful and treacherous 'directions' or, in any case, directions hostile to its own interests. And why should this ever change?"[48] (It should be recalled that in order to demonstrate the non-revolutionary character of the 1968 wildcat general strike, this unruffled and smugly compliant character noted, under one of the pseudonyms he was using back then, that "if you have these unions, a raise of 5% is the most you can get, and if 5% is what you want, these unions suffice" [cf. *I.S.* no. 12]).[49] As for Marxism, "it was predestined to become the natural ideology of bureaucracy. That this Marxism is 'deformed' in relation to Marx's own thought is of absolutely no importance (even if it were true, which is not the case). This is the actual historical Marxism; the other exists at best only between the lines of a few texts."[50]

The nonthinker is, in his own way, rather Hegelian in his glorification of *what exists*: he simply replaces the self-development of Spirit with his own little thoughtless void. Everything leads into it, yet nothing comes out. After thus pacing up and down and elbowing his way around his packed intellectual cell, Castoriadis still wants to play the revolutionary and end on a lyrical note: "The revolutionary project has become such that it will have no meaning or reality if the overwhelmingly majority of men and women who live in contemporary society do not come to assume it and make it the active expression of their needs and desires. There can be no supreme savior and no one category responsible for humanity's fate."[51] This exemplifies the typical modus operandi of the semi-leftist sociologist who, on the one hand, declares the proletariat abolished by virtue of the never-ending hierarchical and wage subdivisions produced by modern capitalism ("The interrelation of all aspects of social life and of the problems that its transformation would pose, does not allow one to define a central and sovereign point that would dominate all others. But the idea of such a point and its identification with production and work is an essential part of the Marxist metaphysics"[52]). Yet this same figure, on the other hand, cannot stop talking about a "revolutionary project," which would not, strictly speaking, fall within the living conditions of "the overwhelming majority of men and women who live in contemporary society," but would instead exist outside them, as nebulous as Castoriadis himself and his declarations of revolutionary intent.

The proletariat is, of course, only a "category" for the ideologist whose professional specialization consists in manipulating such categories, which inverse logic promptly goes on to convince him are the real driving force behind society. Castoriadis shares the same terrain, but at the next stage of decomposition: he sees this driving force at work in the absence of categories, since the destruction of categories is his own specialization as a thinker of nothingness. He says of Marxism that "its attribution of an 'historical mission' to the proletariat is mythical, as is the idea of an historical mission itself, regardless of whoever might bear it."[53] Thus, as if in return for his anti-proletarian rigor, he abandons his own views on a historical mission. Talk about magnanimity! But if Marx assigns to the proletariat the historical role of the class that abolishes all classes, it is not, as Castoriadis seems to believe, because he thinks of proletarians as *gods*. In the proletarianized existence of "the overwhelming majority of men and women who live in contemporary society," humankind has indeed lost itself, but *can* nevertheless acquire the theoretical consciousness of this loss and *must* acquire it, since nothing can satisfy human beings short of the revolutionary reappropriation of their social existence. Of all people, only Castoriadis could be unaware, or pretend to be unaware, that far from identifying this "central and sovereign point"—the unity of proletariat's class consciousness—with "production and labour,"[54] Marxism in actual fact identifies it with the practical negation that leads to the abolition of the existing mode of production, and the abolition of labor.

Castoriadis has definitely not lost much by getting lost, but neither has he ever acquired even the slightest theoretical awareness of this loss. Marx rightly noted that "the propertied class and the class of the proletariat present the same human self-estrangement,"[55] although the former feels at home in this alienation, possessing within it the *appearance* of human existence. What is entirely novel about modern capitalism has been the attempt to give proletarians too the appearance of human existence, to make them feel comfortable in their alienation. We know how little success this has had. What at any rate has dissatisfied the proletariat has been quite enough to satisfy Castoriadis, along with many of those who work in the very sector responsible for producing such appearances. The liquidation of revolutionary Marxism has always greatly exceeded the intellectual means of those who, for nearly a century, have regularly undertaken to carry it out. But never before, it must be said, has this liquidation enjoyed such a consensus among such an incompetent bunch of functionaries. There has clearly been hardly any progress in this area since Eduard Bernstein's "dependence on Hegelian schemas,"[56] etc. But, for his part, Bernstein, in all respects more serious, was pursuing a specific set of practical policies in accordance with a coherent ideology that he himself had formulated. The anti-Marxism of contemporary thinkers merely panders to their own social position and is as patchily applied as it is unstable: thus Castoriadis can now, in the latest installment of his never-ending vacuousness, launch bold attacks on "political thought" that, from Plato to Marx (decidedly inseparable), is "based on an ontology of identity for which *to be* has always meant *to be determinate*" and dream up a "social history" in his own image, a "*magma*" of "imaginary social significations."[57] But this indeterminacy of his "radical imagination," between two interstellar flights of fancy, has nevertheless run into the highly determinate reality of the bureaucrats of the CFDT into whose journal he is now about to discharge his thick gibberish, hot on the heels of Daniel Mothé,[58] the bona fide worker of Socialisme ou Barbarie.

Comprehensive breaking news on this shapeshifting dupe is provided on the back cover of his latest excrement (*The Imaginary Institution of Society*),[59] whose gelatinousness alone would be enough to persuade me, if need be, to consider his case definitively settled: it's a book whose very blurb is enough to *torpedo it*. I'd like to take this opportunity to stipulate that despite the high productivity of recuperators, the present dictionary will not be updated as often as the Larousse. The assessment made here applies to all their future works, which will, I am convinced, endeavor to confirm its accuracy.

Deleuze, Gilles

Dumber than Guattari (see *Guattari, Felix*).

Foucault, Michel

At a time when "the concept of generalized self-management" has become a thesis topic for graduate students (such as Guillerm, now a sociologist specializing in the subject together with Bourdet),[60] it should come as no surprise that the first intellectual doormat to be stepped on, an academic, jabbers on about the most exotic subjects, and even focuses on what tramples all over his utter mediocrity as a civil servant. Such is the case with "criminality," a term under which the authorities and their mass media lump together two concrete aspects of the critique of law and the state: proletarian violence and the barbarism of abundance. The scholar will have no trouble recognizing in this criminality a sign of social crisis, whose meaning and scope it is of course up to him and his colleagues to define. Just as a schoolmaster proves his moral superiority over Alexander the Great by the fact that he has never ventured out and conquered, so the scholar will base the scientific superiority of his interpretations on the fact that he definitely never killed anyone and has always left the world in peace. We thus find Foucault, crafty and windswept (there is a wobbliness about the structure), now talking about crime, illegality, and (why not?) subversion.

The main problem for this new discipline is to maintain its specificity with respect to the researchers working more conventionally on behalf of the police. Given the rather primitive disposition of the latter, this is still, after all, quite easy to achieve. But this due regard for the right to employment also leads these modern criminologists to take a dim view of any criminal who is tactless enough to provide a crystal-clear rationale for their actions. Thus, *Professor* Foucault is censorious of Lacenaire, whose intelligence he finds, quite understandably, highly suspect[61] and thus reason to accuse him of intellectualism; in short, of being a small-time crook. For Foucault, the guardian of popular criminal orthodoxy at the Collège de France, coarser criminals are needed; illiteracy may even be required as a stamp of authenticity, or at least criminals who provide him with the opportunity to peddle his exegetical contortions and tics. Fall into line everyone! He had thus delighted in unearthing the itinerary through the Normandy bocage[62] of an individual who would have been a perfectly respectable and inoffensive country boy were it not for a few members of his family, themselves of an impeccable and upright Freudian orthodoxy. Here, then, is a criminal after his own heart, or rather after police records, who is content merely with a spot of moronic butchery and whose confession to the police had amateur written all over it. Suddenly coming across as a Marxist when touching upon the subject of Lacenaire, Foucault cautions that this criminal is a "ruined petty bourgeois, well educated and literate."[63] On this last point, Foucault's bitterness is perfectly understandable. It will, moreover, come as no surprise that the general drift of this Stalino-academic Marxist waffle, designed exclusively to address awkward details like these, eventually leads him to argue, in the best conspiratorial tradition, that Lacenaire was in cahoots with the police.

§

The latest bluff of separated thought, whose very poverty has been exhausted—in contrast to reality, which is being enriched first and foremost by structuralism's encounter with revolution—consists in placing some dark and mysterious subject of actually existing history somewhere or other (Foucault's "body" or Lyotard's "libidinal economy," or, at another level, Glucksmann's "plebs" or Castoriadis's "autonomy of the proletariat"), a subject whose evanescent but unimpeachable authenticity will ensure that it remains impervious to all rational explanation. A perpetual remake, all in all, of a creaking, cod-philosophical cul-de-sac: "silk stockings . . . the thing in itself too," to quote Duchamp.[64] But far from such excruciating shortcomings triggering a wave of, at the very least, intellectual suicides among these thinkers, they barely stop to draw breath. Indeed, their measly incoherent rumblings are the only indication within academic circles of the unfathomable reality whose murky autonomy they grimly extol against all coherent theory. The crass gimmick being: yes, I am lying, but no more so than anyone else, since truth is inexpressible and only the inexpressible is true. So, they yammer on about discourse, the discourse of power, the power of discourse, etc. (see *Franklin*, the great destroyer of truth). This, as we know, is what Godard had already accomplished at the end of his career (cf. *I.S.* no. 12, p. 104).[65]

What obviously disturbs all these restlessly inquisitive and questionable minds is that, as far as truth is concerned, recent history has already begun to *decide matters*, and the ideas they want to pass off as arbitrary hypotheses and fanciful speculations have begun, by encountering the reality heading their way, to take on the magnitude of a current of social critique that is impossible to *cover up*, as the journalists say. The fine food mongers of falsification may compete with each other to a greater or lesser extent, in order to partake in an extremely limited customer base, but they are all united in support of the spectacular monopoly of social explanation exercised by wall-to-wall mainstream media (of which they are merely a pretentious semi-luxurious accessory, like the impoverished craft industry sector revived by the ever-increasing standardization of products). Like any technician of falsehood on television or in the press, they are exasperated by practical truth which speaks for itself, that is to say, gives no quarter to their charlatanism, since such truth bases its cause on nothing external to its own verificatory activity. They will become all the more hysterical once they get to know the full picture (consider how social barbarism became civilized: Castoriadis, Lefort, Lyotard).

No doubt reluctant to be thus *verified* by the present, Foucault himself plumps for a suitably rather remote past in order to play the talented personality. But neither is he particularly keen on anybody knowing either what his rationale is or on communicating it. Lacenaire therefore becomes "a reassuring character";[66] "despite all his good will, his neophyte's zeal, he was only able to commit, and even then with a singular lack of skill, no more than a few minor crimes";[67] "his fame owed nothing either to the extent of his crimes or to the art of their conception; it was their ineptitude that gave cause for surprise."[68] Foucault should know. But his embarrassing intellectual misery has simply not understood what Lacenaire's crime was.

It is well known that, at the end of the last research phase undertaken by modern art, which led it to become nothing more than private collections of works, the Dada movement resorted to the technique of scandal, which reversed the situation by bringing the public together *shorn of artworks* in order to confront it with the liquidation of art. For his part, the criminal wishing to crown his work with the public glow of well-merited glory finds himself stripped of it by his very success, which tends to condemn him to a certain anonymity. This incidentally explains the "compulsion to confess," about which a Freudian nobody by the name of Reik filled a large volume of drivel.[69] No doubt criminals prior to Lacenaire could expect to obtain some publicity by virtue of the cynical frankness of their confessions, which their act had not secured by itself. Yet Lacenaire was the first to reverse the situation so masterfully by raising the confession to the rank of a major crime. He carried out a few cheap and nasty murders only as a prelude to the scandal of this trial: "If you could have read my heart, you would have read its inner thought of self-destruction, but self-destruction that should blaze forth as a lesson to the part of Society which I represented in 1829 when they denied me a place at the feast" (*Mémoires*).[70] And it was precisely in this particular admission that the scandalized authorities saw the real danger, so much so that the police, in order to discredit his "incredible frankness,"[71] circulated a fake account of his execution, according to which his last moments saw him behave like a coward before the guillotine.

"You said it yourselves, you men of Justice, . . . 'Society will be avenged.' And I said to myself, 'Society will be struck to the heart.'"[72] Lacenaire spoke in the name of *the bad side* of society, and had this bad side clearly emerge as the side that struggles and makes history—whereas up to that point it had only emerged, through the utopians and social reformers, as *the good side*, which believed that historical evil could be promptly and effortlessly transcended in order to achieve reconciliation and harmony. It would not be until June 1848 that the sentence passed by Lacenaire on society began to gather the means for its execution.

Thus, contrary to the Stalinoid platitude according to which Lacenaire was no revolutionary, the focus should be on how he was the bearer of what the revolutionaries of his time still lacked. As a case in point, the savagery of his black humor, far from being some kind of outdated aestheticism, is nowadays so topical that the tiny Foucault will soon feel the weight of it, as demonstrated by the story, which appeared in the daily *France-Soir* on July 17, 1974, of an *extreme case* of increasingly widespread Monday morning sabotage: "'In keeping with the WXLT practice of presenting the most immediate and complete reports of local blood and guts news, TV 40 presents what is believed to be a television first. In living color, an exclusive coverage of an attempted suicide.' And sure enough, Christine Chubbuck, 30, the pretty news anchor for one of the television stations in Sarasota, Florida, pulled a revolver from a drawer and, in front of tens of thousands of viewers watching on Monday morning, shot herself in the head."

§

To finish with Foucault, it should be noted that the reader will perhaps doubt that it is even worth hating or indeed vilifying somebody who, despite all his efforts to mix with the riffraff, will always remain a self-righteous numbskull. To justify myself on this point alone, I should mention that I have never read a single one of this man's books, nor those of his colleagues in general, but that I happened, while distractedly leafing through his latest one (*Discipline and Punish*) in a bookshop—and just as boredom was beginning to put me to sleep—to come across the above-discussed gem about Lacenaire, which woke me up. I did not feel of a mind, naturally, to undertake my own assessment of the rest of the volume's jewelry, aware of the public's lack of interest in tawdry junk. Nor can I be reproached for giving too much consideration to this professorial nonsense, because after all, accidentally stepping in a piece of shit on your way out of the house is not the same as deliberately kicking it.

Franklin, Jean

Piling them up in a motley assortment of worm-eaten antiques (vestiges of the old ultra-leftism), the evergreen junkmonger called *10/18* [éditions Dix-Dix-Huit] juxtaposes unquestionably second-hand schlock (anthologies of articles from the journal *Cause Commune*, edited by erstwhile *Arguments* editor Jean Duvignaud,[73] or even an absurd "Journal of Aesthetics"[74]), alongside bits of novelties mass-produced in some Hong Kong–esque intellectual sweatshop.[75] Here the whole uselessness of today, yesterday, and tomorrow merges into a single mass of worthless rubbish, where Maoisms and Hoxhaisms are kitsch jokes, where potboilers double as serious scientific research, and a Bordigist hack cannibalizes "Marx-Engels" into digest-sized scraps to the point of making Marx and Engels look like the Fantômas thriller coauthors Souvestre and Allain.[76] Thanks to the confusion, the Marquis de Sade has at least made his way onto train station bookshelves, a move that constitutes the only saving grace of this eclecticism.

Certainly, there have always been books designed more to be displayed than read. But when not displayed for their market value (like those bound books that doctors purchase by the meter), it used to be for their recognized cultural prestige, like the literature of Sartre or Camus, then Lévi-Strauss or Robbe-Grillet, which the student of the 1960s had to have prominently on show.

But with the rapid erosion of all cultural prestige, forbidden from forming by excessive advertising, worthless and mundane books are now *directly* produced to be displayed among the accoutrements of the advanced spectator. (If the transformation from student to junior manager has already taken place, they can purchase the *Encyclopaedia Universalis* on credit, which offers the same old, albeit more luxuriously packaged, authors—Castoriadis, Lefort, Baudrillard, Glucksmann, Attali, etc.) And of course, the manufacturing of these products meets all the requirements of the paltry use for which they are intended: their authors write as they are read and pretend to think just as their readers will pretend to read them.

Returning to *10/18*, this great collector of the sewage of recuperative thinking monopolizes a good half of the miasma inventoried here. Registering the last groans and hiccups of beleaguered confusionism from Vincennes to Cerisy[77] and from one interminable seminar after another, it is feverishly building up the archives of contemporary nonsense into a time bomb for cold posterity. (Even that clown René Viénet and his wordplay are in the anti-Maoist sinology section.) There is undoubtedly a commendable self-denial in all of this, and a disinterestedness that is quite rare among publishers, since the public seems not to be showing any of the expected scientific interest in these archaeological excavations into the underbelly of the Zeitgeist. Yet its laziness is now rewarded: it will be easier and more pleasant for the public to read the present work to find out how recuperation is progressing.

As self-denial or stupidity, recuperation has in any case allowed us to observe the flash of a new unidentified flying object in the sky of modernized imbecility; unidentified, because he is probably no more Franklin than the other is Manchette, which is not to say that they're the same. But if it's not him, it's his brother,[78] that is to say, any one of the two-bit charlatans eager to cover their philosophy exam papers in "radical critique" whitewash. The wonders of painstaking rewriting— smacking of the intellectual zoo at Vincennes since Lacanian gimmicks stink of a freshly escaped hyena—thus furnish us with the following revelations on *Le discours du pouvoir*: "Effectively reined in and understood in its temporal and historical, albeit supra-historicist, determinations, language works to *reproduce* the social organization whose humble and endlessly pliable underling it is; it is what turns into the discourse of the order of power, belonging to this order insofar as it serves and fosters its preservation and ascendancy, etc., etc."[79] I will spare the reader any more in the same vein up to the bitter end, trusting that this stream of waffle will collapse under its own weight and sink into the quicksand of its own vacuousness. Franklin's ruminations here are nevertheless true to their object, "understood in its temporal and historical determinations" in the shape of standardized, suitably conspicuous academic fare.

In short, as was pointed out back in 1963, just when Franklin was about to begin studying philosophy before going on to university, where he would pick up the intellectual offcuts that he is now putting to such fruitful use: "Words *work*."[80] Under Franklin's pen, the poor things must even have to work flat out for the purpose of turbocharging his pathetic bluff. He thus sets about breathing new life into Joseph Gabel, in order to demonstrate the trenchancy of his own critical intransigence toward such an adversary.[81] Given that his discussions of the writings of any old garden-variety Lyotard, Deleuze, or Baudrillard are conducted in a spirit of urbane academic politeness, the bombast he deploys with regard to the obvious limitations of Gabel's work is particularly comical. But Gabel's work, published *in 1962*, then had a usefulness that a *gadget* and total marketing dummy like Franklin could not even imagine. His signal impudence (he already sees himself pursuing a risk-free career out of Gabel's skin) even prompts him to scoff at the latter's adoption of Mannheim's sociological category of the *socially unattached intelligentsia*; thus, not for one moment does the unintelligent and demonstrably attached Franklin believe that Mannheim's category could denote and encompass the historical reality of a specific *déclassé* social group to which Marx as well as Bakunin and many others belonged. And moreover, even today, although under very different conditions, such a semi-clandestine reality exists whereby most of those who could easily find employment and succeed in the cultural sphere have no wish to, while those eagerly marketing themselves, like Franklin, have only trifles to offer. But if he has never been concerned with unattached intelligence, neither has he ever been given an *easy ride*.

Franklin's extremism has less of a swagger to it when he wants to show off and parade around at the expense of more consequential adversaries than Gabel, in which case he prefers more often than not to remain cautiously vague. "Some," "a few," have spoken of truth and falsehood, rational and irrational, consciousness and illusion. This is all terribly *passé*. "It is time to dissolve the entities." Indeed, "the dialectic fails as soon as it tackles psychic functioning" (evidence, incidentally, of a hackneyed Castoriadisism). So, "revolution is also beyond truth and falsehood as well as good and evil,"[82] and Franklin, who was the first to issue a fatwa against truth and falsehood, consciousness, and everything else, is unquestionably in the vanguard of this ongoing revolution. But he is not entirely alone, given the arrival of reinforcements in the shape of an old, worn-out, grumbling yet stubborn and faithful campaign veteran, whom Franklin quotes glowingly in his dispatch: "We can only applaud [the idiot already speaks like a head of state] the eagerness shown by Baudrillard ['remember, grenadier, when the sun rose over Austerlitz-Nanterre'[83]] for the rejection he salvages [from the dustbin of inquisitiveness] of a determinism regarding 'objective conditions' where revolt becomes expectation."[84] For the sheer intellectual complaisance, we can only applaud the sight of Baudrillard and Franklin refusing to admit that their dismal chatter is quite simply determined by their "objective condition" as miserable thinkers for hire. Indeed, their smug impatience *brooks no delay* in turning submissiveness into some sociology lectureship based in the suburbs as a prelude to propel oneself from conference to conference across the globe, on the heels of that survivor of all the Bérézinas[85] of thought Henri Lefebvre who, according to the blurb accompanying his latest philosophical marmalade (*Hegel, Marx, Nietzsche: Or, The Realm of Shadows*), "travels the world trying to achieve global thinking." Keep on running! If ever Lefebvre's mind does lift off into cosmic overdrive, he will surely achieve planetary orbit. In the meantime, what remains of his thinking is running out of steam ahead of Beijing, and so he "declares himself 'pro-China,' therefore 'strategically Maoist.'" (He confides in us about his "love story" with the Situationists, "that ended badly, very badly."[86] Poor thing!) As for Franklin, his rate of obsolescence is such that he stands no chance of entertaining us for as long as Lefebvre. But he nonetheless stays on track by proudly concluding his book with the chapter, "At Last, the Urban": "Here we reach what will have been understood as the *basis* of the discourse of power and the locus of its development."[87] The *senectitude* here reeks from the ground up to high heaven.

The rackets of impatient cultural wannabes like Franklin are obviously all sworn enemies of Marxist analysis, which these dimwits find crude. But even in its most vulgar application, this analytical approach is still fairly adequate and appropriate to its object, especially when the object is these imbeciles. Thus their professional degeneration as producers of shoddy cultural commodities has them turn their immediate fire on Marxism, since they judge everything only in terms of fashion; they believe that they are done once and for all with the theory of revolution, since they see no trace of it in the marketplace, which is seasonally swamped by the latest consignment of their confusionism, whether of the home-grown, Stalinist, or leftist variety that serves as their foil.

But let's take a closer look at Franklin's lightning program to sweep away objective conditions and their untimely determinism: "It is above all a question of breaking down structures and balances of investment, of demobilizing energy and increasing a distribution of desire, which will not emerge from supplications to its concept."[88] Hey Franklin, it is too late in the Lyotardian century for you to start dreaming of going anywhere on the basis of your moth-eaten gimmicks, since there are far more experienced charlatans than you around who already run the well-structured "libidinal economy" racket. The concoction you whipped up is all for nothing. Your fifteen minutes are up.

When not critically decorating fragments of philosophy and philosophically rewriting fragments of critique, this disciple of nothingness pompously declares elsewhere: "A path has to be found, a strategy has to be invented,"[89] in the pioneering tone now adopted by all the stragglers dawdling behind recuperation, who would like to be given the time to make the most of the two or three little gimmicks they picked up along the way. But Franklin's path is plain to see, although he lags far behind Lyotard, who discovered that "underneath their twentieth-century Saint-Simonian style, [the Situationists had] a solid attachment to Hegelianism, and therefore to Christianity."[90] Thus, just as it is necessary for his scholastic speculations to have some content from time to time, and for this charade of a "leftist critique" to give some idea of its critical stance, Franklin—after touching on the "coincidence of the structuring of the ego with ideology" and "concerning the ideological/non-ideological opposition, it is not and never is a question of truth or falsehood"—finally comes to the point: "The 'ideologization' of revolutionary theory—if it can be posited as an absolutely pure ideological construct—which Debord strives to explain, also originates there. Neither intellectual deficiency, nor practical inadequacy, nor even some 'nondescript' life (and even less some ontological 'disability') will do as explanations, however much they impinge on this moment."[91] Thus anybody reading Franklin can learn about the existence of revolutionary theory only by the announcement of its burial, yet will be able to console themselves against this distressing news by structuring their ego ideologically, although this will certainly require something more consistent than what Franklin is offering here.

As for the "ideologization" of revolutionary theory, over which Franklin sheds his crocodile tears, it can find its origins anywhere, at the level of analysis where he places himself, in the structuring of the ego, or a fractious adolescence, exactly like his own imbecility, which has undoubtedly undergone a long development before reaching its current, full-blown maturity. But this kind of *analysis* interests only those who get paid for carrying it out, and whose customer base Franklin, like others, envies. For their part, the "explanations" to which he refers (*The Real Split in the International: Theses on the Situationist International and Its Time*) instead dealt with the conditions of social existence that allow and maintain a certain ideological use of some of the impoverished results of revolutionary theory by a stratum of spectators whose disability was in no way ontological, but part and parcel of their social development as petty cadres and managers buttressed by *their acceptance* of this development—an acceptance for which all intellectual shortcomings and practical inadequacies find a perfect breeding ground.[92] "Ideologization" is a big word to describe their short-lived enthusiasm and the subsequent frustration that it never worked the wonders expected of it. When his loudmouthing turned sour, the *pro-situ* started fulminating against everything of which he had been enamored the day before, all the more easily since it had never meant the slightest thing to him: history, theory, the proletariat no longer exist and perhaps never did. Having conquered this summit of disillusioned thinking, the *pro-situ* undertook the last judgment on all past and future revolutions: workers' councils merely deceive workers; the *pro-situ* is smarter, and self-management only a miserable trap that treacherously perverts subversive truth whose omnipresence, moreover, he must at the same time affirm and whose one and only meaning he holds an exclusive monopoly over. At this point he is ready and willing to accompany decomposing academic thought into its dustbin. Yet the *pro-situ* will have difficulty carving out a place there, since it's already swarming with emptiness more swollen than he. That all this decay has little to do with any ideologization is never more apparent than when reading Franklin. His pretentious conceptualizations—he maintains that "discourse of power" is a concept— which have gone entirely unnoticed in the congestion of pseudo-thinking, are fairly representative of the career that this kind of vacuous extremism can expect, and typical of its careerist misery. The failure of what Franklin is saying to be even heard is a caricature of the emptiness of extremism at a time when reality itself leads to more extremes than will ever be found in the heads of philosophers, however big-headed they become.

In one of his moments of euphoria, after announcing that his plan is not to become a dialectician (no kidding), Franklin takes vituperation to such an extreme that he declares that "the joke about 'the communication of theory' is no longer funny,"[93] a statement that speaks volumes about the author of these amusements. However, the conceptual dandyish attitude of false cynicism that he parades around is not very convincing, and since he is unable to put his money where his mouth is, he prefers to hide behind a pseudonym. He will now have to find another one in order to regain his street credibility, or even just to *redirect* the attention that I have drawn to "Franklin" by my rescuing him from oblivion. Something along the lines of a lightning rod would be my suggestion, in order to divert thunderbolts by adopting the name of some imbecile or other whose existence is a joke that nobody finds funny anymore: let's say, for instance, a name like François George.[94]

Glucksmann, André

Back in the day, the earnest and hopelessly agog Glucksmann carved out something of a reputation for himself for his sterling ability to lump together, with a straight face, Machiavelli, Clausewitz, and Mao, with the theory of the first two stoking the radiant thoughts (*sic*) of the third. May 1968 had very obviously consigned him, along with a few other strategists of similar caliber, to deserved oblivion. After marinating for some time in leftist broth, he then made a sensational comeback as a heartbreaker of Marxism: no prizes here for originality, of course, but since Glucksmann is more photogenic than all the other conceptually and concupiscently challenged has-beens, he now has the green light to proceed. Deliquescent leftist intellectual circles thus jumped at this golden opportunity to be able to hear nothing more about Marxism except its eulogy: everything must be reassessed, and that is precisely what these circles are here to do.

That someone as radically disqualified as Glucksmann can talk about anything important without arousing general outrage should hardly surprise us, considering that more conspicuous scum than him still have *carte blanche* to lie with impunity (were a Stalinist to be instanced here, the phenomenal Elleinstein, a historian on orders from the PCF to examine the "Stalinist phenomenon," would be a case in point).[95] But it should be noted that in his lack of dignity, Glucksmann is well below those ruined capitalists who threw themselves out of windows in 1929, never for his part been driven to commit suicide by the collapse of ideology: his brand new schtick comprising the sprucing up of his literary stock, where the masses who no longer serve as material on which to hold forth about the "people's war," will at least serve as corpses on which to discuss our own iron century, whose Marxism has turned out to be such a disappointment to him.

Let us take a closer look at the great discoveries of this skunk by following him along the road to Damascus where he encountered anti-Marxism. Accomplishing the daring feat of appearing even more moronic than he actually is, he pretends to have suddenly realized, upon reading the works of Solzhenitsyn,[96] that there was a totalitarian bureaucracy in Russia, whose police terror was inseparable from ideological absolutism. Having apparently had no prior warning of such a revelation from any corner of his leftist comfort zone, where the policing is strictly ideological, he is left sputtering with outrage: so, the bureaucrats are lying! (But just as he is not really surprised, his outrage rings hollow, its sycophantic ranting as gutless as the customary cynicism of the vile *Charlie Hebdo* that it nevertheless holds in abeyance during election time to call for a vote for Mitterrand.)

All this would be of no interest whatsoever were it not for the fact that it stands as further testimony to modern-day revolutionary impetuousness that, alongside more significant transformations, could even raise the intellectual level of a Maoizer like Glucksmann if, as might be expected following such a traumatic sea change, he actually did venture to shake up his thinking in response to wholly new stimuli. Not Glucksmann though. No doubt burning to share his excitement, he immediately churns out some two hundred pages (*La cuisinière et le mangeur d'hommes*[97]) in which the launch of his above-mentioned discovery provides endless scope for his inquisitiveness via a farrago of moth-eaten lyricism and 1950s schoolboy humor. His unadulterated iconoclastic fury spares nothing and nobody: he attacks Marx, but also Hegel, and even—unconscionably—Plato.

After such an intellectual earthquake, which surely must have shaken final-year philosophy textbooks to their core, Glucksmann is by no means alone amongst the ruins: he still has Mao. His customary devastating disrespect stops at the ridiculous Chinese bureaucracy, which is nevertheless more accessible in every single respect than Plato. He doubts but remains undaunted. A further ten years may, however, serve to alter that if he continues his intellectual progress apace and should he ever receive from China a damning first-hand account of another few million extra deaths.

In the meantime, he plays down the only bit of gumption he has with paper-thin humility: a shameless liar, he thusly writes: "in the eyes of Russian camp survivors, their relatives, those currently locked away in

KGB-run psychiatric asylums and Gulag denizens, we come across as inexorably stupid."[98] (Speak for yourself Glucksmann, speak for yourself. Although it is doubtful that the light of André Glucksmann's thinking will ever reach Siberia, it is certain that this trash would not even survive the trip to Vorkuta, let alone the Siberian Gulag.[99] This studied insolence is custom-made for the Parisian intellectual rabble who feign titillation.) Then this, further down on the same page: "Those troubled by the Czech resistance are unaffected by Western protest movements [is our intrepid thinker actually about to discover how censorship works? No, his sights are set much farther afield], as if the Czech events were merely a performance where clumsy actors parade around in 1917 costumes on the trestles of some wax museum."[100] It is certainly the case that the absurd Leninist pretensions of Western leftism (for which, it is safe to say, judging from his silence on the matter, the clumsy Glucksmann intends to remain one of the poster boys) are of no concern to those who put up with the Stalinist truth of Leninism on an eminently practical and daily basis. But in a precisely reverse and proportional way to Ratgeb (see entry below), Glucksmann merely hopes to use the cover of generalized stupidity to hide his own specific stupidity, in this day and age when not everyone has been so stupid, or indeed, so Glucksmannish.

For Glucksmann, between a muddled and cagey 1949 editorial by the Sartre and Merleau-Ponty double act,[101] whose "rare lucidity" he praised, to his own light bulb moment in 1975, Stalinism remained a constant. He then rubbed his eyes and woke up. He would like us to believe that everyone was sleeping at the same time as him. This sleeping beauty, whose prince charming was Solzhenitsyn the priest, is presented to us as a "Maoist philosopher." From his master he learned the impudence of falsification, yet he still lacks the power to correct history philosophically. The left-wing press does what it can to make up for it: "The whole history of the post-May period is a chronicle of a slow but radical schism between the far left and Marxism; a schism to which a few recent books already bear witness [there follow the titles of six pieces of nonsense, three of which are published in a book series edited by the verbose hack Lévy himself]. All of them have Maoism in common, all thereby contributing to that uncompromising and heroic trajectory that could well destabilize our erstwhile political consciousness" (Bernard-Henri Lévy writing in *Le Nouvel Observateur*).[102] The erstwhile political consciousness of this little-known historian will never be grasped with any certainty, but we suspect that it "could well" change dramatically every week to the rhythm of the intellectual flavor of the month of the rag that employs him, since his "uncompromising and heroic trajectory" led him the following week to pay homage to the Marxist and academic prowess of the Stalinist Althusser.

But let us return to real history. Staying with France and those dark years of intellectual submissiveness whose perfect representative was Sartre with his inimitable way of overcoming his scruples and caving into the Stalinists, from 1949 onward the critique of bureaucratic countries was being developed in the pages of *Socialisme ou Barbarie*. There is no way, however, that this could come as news to the Glucksmann rummaging through Sartrean bric-a-brac (by now well chilled and from all accounts available in paperback, mortal remains serving as material for Castoriadis to endlessly mull over in one of his interminable prefaces, which in turn gave Glucksmann the idea for his above-mentioned Stalino-Platonic guff). No possible news either to Sartre, now daring to say that he was pro-Stalinist for so long because there was nothing to the left of the Stalinists: spoken like a true lackey who sees only what power shows him as the only power that could possibly exist. It is true that among all the other tidbits piously assembled by *Le Nouvel Observateur* is a declaration by Sartre that he has always been an anarchist. And just as Marx is now a Stalinist, then surely Sartre can be an anarchist, and Glucksmann fearless. His Mitterrandism now turning sour, the *Nouvel Observateur* hack Jean Daniel can, after all, now be found extolling the sycophantic Mário Soares's "libertarian tendencies."[103]

In this night where all ruminations of thought are suddenly as black as anarchy,[104] it is just a matter of taking the bull by the horns to ask: who are these people and what have they done in the face of the momentous challenges imposed by the era? They think they can introduce their little historical revisions through the backdoor simply because they are *oblivious* to the possibility of anybody holding them accountable, just as they are *oblivious* to anything on the left of the Communist Party or the grotesque Gauche prolétarienne (GP).[105] The Glucksmann school of confusionism thus naturally elicits a shower of superlatives from Pierre Daix,[106] one Stalinist not averse to a makeover who, in addition to a 1975 authorized biography, is getting a de-Stalinized mausoleum ready for Louis Aragon. (This bastard, whose days are numbered and who knows it, first launched his own embalming process in 1970 under the aegis of one Alain Jouffroy who rattles on about "revolutionary individualism" as the "multiplication of oneself,"[107] undoubtedly because he himself could be multiplied an incalculable number of times and still remain minuscule, but who more prosaically joined the May 29, 1968 Communist Party—CGT protest march in the company of his new master Aragon[108]—Breton was dead so Jouffroy could go guzzling in the deepest trough without having to look over his shoulder—thus adding his own insignificance to those of Godard, Sollers, and a few other relics of imperiled modernism. Jouffroy thus used the pretext of a preface in order to pimp corpses and to reconcile Breton postmortem with someone he despised until the end, even asserting that nothing really separated Breton and Aragon, that the two were "paradoxically" united, etc.: two sides of a coin he was in a hurry to spend.)

It is understandable that Aragon finds his surrealist past more prestigious than his Stalinist present,[109] however decomposed it may be—just as Glucksmann prefers to talk more about Plato than about his Maoism, however deliquescent it may be. The mediocre erudition of the first Rubel to come along can, moreover, be expected to carry out the painstaking job of bringing together umpteen quotations from Marx himself and bits of Marxist ideology for the edification of readers versed only in the Maoist Marx. As is beginning to become apparent, the *simple* method favored by the thought of history, which alone has access to the truth of its past because it can grasp the possible use of it in the here and now, is to usher in its practical conditions of existence by clearly opposing all falsifiers. In the course of a somewhat hasty commendation of a kind of intellectual Yalta that would leave him and his ilk to administer their own artistic and cultural lower-tier jurisdiction in peace, the loathsome Jouffroy wrote: "Between Aragon and Breton, never again will there be a choice."[110] While Jouffroy's ecumenism may commandeer the dead and pacify the graveyards, it will not alter the fact that an increasing number of the living are *choosing* to spit on him, and on everything for which he stands.

Between great discoveries and small falsifications, all these lies are closely interrelated. Naturally combining stupidity with vulgarity, Glucksmann attracts attention only through the hype around his self-confession as a disillusioned leftist: this inane little undertaking is the exoteric, mass-market version of the more sophisticated antihistorical shenanigans that the Castoriadis–Lefort double act and its followers confidentially engage in. No doubt trying to conceal his game, Glucksmann extols the ancestral virtues of the peasantry and even seems to think that he stands on the eve of a new peasants' revolt; he also talks in the majestic ecumenical plural about "our religions," mentions "the Resistance" alongside May 1968 among the "great moments," with the same truly *Stalinist* nostalgia that led his friends in the Gauche Prolétarienne to lay wreaths on Mont Valérien,[111] and haphazardly piles up events that have called Marxism into question: "the revolutions of the 'third world,' the Cultural Revolution in China, Western protest movements, the revolt of Portuguese captains."[112] This populism, tinted with an anarchism that bleats for Larzac,[113] thus reaches out to the priests, patriots, and the military, and smacks of a vote-grabbing exercise targeting provincial bigots who learn from *Le Figaro* that they must read an "astonishing book" of this fine young man whose soul has been saved by Solzhenitsyn.[114] But Glucksmann's actual readership is nevertheless on the left, even on the extreme left, where short shrift is given across the board to what, as revolutionary theory, never would or could be of any use, and, as ideology, to what amounts to flogging a dead horse.

At a time when totalitarian powers only survive as *comprador* bureaucracies supplying Western capitalism with raw materials, cheap labor, and markets (just like the post-Maoist bureaucracy in China was rescued, for the time being, by oil), the Russian revolution *to come* will return the intellectual semi-opposition and petitioning activities of Sakharovian imbeciles,[115] who virtuously appeal to the West, to its true historical perspective. Already in Russia the ferment of dissolution, introduced with the penetration of commodity abundance, totally at odds with existing ideological absolutism, provokes struggles within the ruling class, whose slide into overt crisis will give the signal for fresh proletarian unrest. The joke will then be on all the Solzhenitsyns who seem important only because real opposition to the Russian bureaucracy has not yet arisen. As for Glucksmann, he needs no such historical light in order to be seen for what he really is: ridiculous and a charlatan.

Guattari, Felix

Dumber than Deleuze (see *Deleuze, Gilles*).

Guégan, Gérard

Contrary to the impression that his stupefying provincialism and boorishness as the Jonny-come-lately of what now goes by the name of culture may have given to ill-informed spectators, Gérard Guégan should not be mistaken for Godard's literary front man. There is no denying, however, that Guégan has been praising Godard, which, for an unscrupulous charlatan like Guégan, is a strange concession to an outdated fashion. Yet numerous television appearances seem to prove the existence, so to speak, of an autonomous fungus named Guégan. For example, he can be found on air in the company of a certain Michel Lancelot, who proudly declared in the columns of the sleazy *Libération* (a dumping ground of decaying leftism) that he wanted to be "recuperated";[116] no doubt thinking that this crude ploy would lead everyone to believe that something in his activities was worthy of recuperation in the first place, and that, in a spirit of Christian sacrifice, he was devoting himself heroically to infiltrating enemy ranks. This kamikaze Lancelot nevertheless leaves behind a work to perpetuate his memory; a work devoted to the "counter culture,"[117] where his stupidity is nevertheless leavened with the superiority he enjoys over hacks Edgar Morin or Jean-François Revel[118] of having managed to grasp that the ideological melting-pot of the American New Left, over which they are ecstatic, is nothing but a degraded and confusing rehash of *every* twentieth-century European avant-garde—from Dadaism to the Situationist International. Lancelot, whose main informant for modern times seems to be the walking lie detector Jean-Louis Brau,[119] naturally gives prominence to the Lettrists but also, at a considerable remove, gives some insight into "the young bourgeois Situationists like Debord," who, after leading a lengthy sybaritic existence "in a large villa above Cannes" and discovering Lettrism "when he was just a young philosophy student," "headed for the North Cape" and on his return "tried to commit suicide,"[120] no doubt in despair at his failure to set up the top-secret base in Lapland that the Kiruna miners were counting on for their eventual liberation of the first territory under the control of Arctic Circle workers' councils.[121]

Writing his "Scenes of Parisian Subversion"[122] on the basis of similarly sourced information (cheap gossip and stereotyped fantasies), although there is some evidence to suggest that he has indeed read the catalog of Éditions Champ Libre, Guégan nevertheless subjects this tittle-tattle to smarter, literary treatment in his capacity as Lancelot's Merlin the Magician. Although he may well miss the "1920s–40s, when everything underwent massive change and writers reflected this in their work," he himself is nothing more than a paltry and hopeless repetition of the literary fraud Malraux—he wouldn't even make it as an elevator operator at the Ministry of Culture, not only because the public today is somewhat less blinkered about revolution, but also because he is imprudent enough to set his novels in Paris and not in Shanghai or North Cape.

However, Guégan, who introduces a kind of "epistemological break" in the work of Godard (described by Guégan as "modern," before the spinelessness of Godard "bent to the dominant ideology"), has set his sights more prosaically on filling the void left by this shyster, now a hostage to leftism and provincialism. Whereas Godard targeted the smug, totally ignorant, and wildly impressionable pre–May 1968 spectator (particularly its student archetype), Guégan instead addresses the ashamed, post–1968 spectator, who is just as pig ignorant but inured to every modernism and nauseated by the political and cultural ersatz mass produced for him. Where Godard would string bits of industrial culture trivia together, Guégan stacks up oddities, second-rate authors, and B-list absurdities in accordance with a kind of tried-and-tested snobbery that consists of arbitrarily talking up curiosities and giving the impression that you own everything else.

But the very specific spice that Guégan uses to season his literary output remains the greatest puzzle for today's catatonic spectator: revolutionary practice, on the extreme fringes of which his protagonists are supposed to exist. A cock-and-bull chronicler of ultra-leftism, this latter-day Ponson du Terrail[123] painstakingly strings together establishment clichés, inventorying conventions of the nonconformist role with a mix of clumsiness and false flippancy that might even be mistaken for an attempt at parody, were it not so obvious that he takes his work completely seriously, as evidenced by his grotesque "ideas" column ("Conjuguer le présent") for *Le Monde*, where he has the "modern ideas monger" François Bott under his boot.[124] As for his attempt to "mash up every facet of today's unruliness and free-spiritedness,"[125] the very essence of Guégan and the key to the minor success he enjoys among a circumscribed audience lies in the only liberty he can take with the truth, that is to say, first and foremost his post as a literary hack and in his reluctance, masquerading as insolence, to grossly contradict his past bombast and lies: along with the watchful herd, he gets to tell everybody that following "re-immersion in *Socialisme ou Barbarie* or the discovery of Marx's *Grundrisse*," "we took to the streets to set things right," although elsewhere we learn from him that prior to 1968 he languished away as a PCF apparatchik, no doubt reading and rereading *Socialisme ou Barbarie*. Further on, he asseverates that "we are tired of serving,"[126] which is rich coming from a literary gofer whom Stalinism has been busily shunting around from one publishing house to another. In the course of Guégan's novels, "various authorial *voices*" cause a scandal on television or have Aragon appear on a street corner;[127] Guégan himself turns actor to play a character in a television adaptation of a screenplay by the Stalinist André Stil,[128] perhaps because the Stalinist Aragon once referred to Stil as "the Stendhal of our time," which, according to François Bott, is a distinction that applies equally from now on to Gérard Guégan, which in turn amounts to saying that Guégan is the André Stil of our time, even though there is no way that Bott himself could claim to be the Aragon of our time. More amusing still, after circulating press releases that he "quit" the publishing house Champ Libre that he "founded" (we took to Easy Street), he admits in his most recent novel that he was simply "sacked," "fired," "dismissed." Maybe he'll tell us why in his next novel.[129]

His cover is blown: this character is such that he would pay to sell himself. It is moreover easy to see why the "revolutionaries" that Guégan portrays in his novels are just about as flimsy as his knowledge of the subject. This clown has his unconvincing marionettes casually talk theory over shots of brandy or "fizzy Chablis" in a bar "off the beaten track" from tourists in conversation that oozes with sentences excerpted from Vaneigem's recent beyond-the-grave preface to a work by Ernest Cœurderoy,[130] before the former's wandering soul was reincarnated as Ratgeb. The reader of Guégan's *Les Irréguliers* even comes close to being shaken out of their stupor when, in the following scene, one of the book's characters rightly points out that "it may be time to leap into the unknown and stop talking about theory."[131] But this leap into the unknown turns out to be nothing more than a relapse into something even more ramshackle, that is, a Manchette-style, hard-boiled crime novel, except that since we are discussing terrorism, "Vendetta" replaces "Nada."[132] For something to pass the time on the train, though, you could do worse than Manchette (less literary pretentiousness).

Guégan has of course never met a revolutionary, theorist or otherwise, since a revolutionary is defined, among other things, by their refusal to associate with people like him. He therefore has to resort to imaginative ploys with results, as we have seen, that go no further than the level of a hip junior manager who reads *Actuel*.[133] Whenever he introduces a "theorist"—a thunderbolt of revolution whose existence seems to haunt his apprentice terrorists—into one of his novelistic routines, it inevitably brings to mind the Prince de Bourbon-Condé's remarks to the Cardinal de Retz concerning the hacks of yore: "impertinent authors, who being born as one may say in the outer court, and having never reached further than the anti-chamber, yet pretend to know everything that passes in the closet": "these wretches have represented both you and me, such as they would have been themselves, if they had been in our posts."[134]

Mixing the remains and pieces of an antediluvian mythology, Guégan is nevertheless careful not to get too involved: he coats everything in his trademark feeble, ersatz humor, a popular form of the old black humor now prevalent even in high schools, which has made parody the intellectual default position for morons, and which simply expresses the general decomposition wrought by the spectacle, with the smug consumption of this downgrading seeking to pass itself off as casualness. In the wake of the technique of collage (downgrading with no upgrade to a higher level), there is kitsch, the accumulation of elements that were already worthless, or that never had any worth to begin with. The dire resuscitation of the novel—a form that became obsolete long before he could even read—attempted here by Guégan is itself part of the snobbery inherent in kitsch: since there are art galleries today that exhibit television sets from the 1950s, why not put novels and Guégans on display as well? Meanwhile, half-pints declare Joyce bourgeois, just as others call Marx reactionary. But one cannot escape one's fate, or, in this case, decomposition: having collapsed his ultra-leftist vein, Guégan is now reduced to padding out the "cut-up technique" of Burroughs,[135] who, fifty years after Tzara's instructions for "writing a Dadaist poem," continues to dangle cut-up sentences pulled out of a hat in the hope of producing something new.

After trying his hand at theory under the name Cloarec, and at Stalinist history under the name Le Braz,[136] Guégan eventually fell back on a mundane literary career in which he is already struggling to move up in the world, hence freelancing for *Le Monde* or *Le Magazine Littéraire*. With so much effort and so many instances of groveling, perhaps he will land the job of filmmaker to which he so aspires: judging by the sheer amount of bootlicking he does, he won't go out of fashion in the process, like Godard. Guégan will be washed up before he begins. He can always rely on Manchette to write a script for him, unless of course his current role as ultimate darling on Lancelot's television shows turns out to be the sum total of his media trajectory.

Lyotard, Jean-François

Lichtenberg told of a man who experienced sudden and violent erections whenever he composed a piece of criticism. Without going into the more or less arousing nature of critical theory, let us note that a new school of thinkers has, however, made a name for itself today by declaring that smug apologetics is much sexier. Lyotard, an expert on the subject, is its leader. He has already been quoted several times in the present work since, in his baseness, he excels in saying aloud what remains shameful to many of his colleagues. He has, moreover, better than others, a quite exceptional, subliterary talent for using up leftovers and making mountains of inanity out of microscopic molehills, activities that Sartre was famous for in his time. Because he looks destined for some increase in popularity, the subject of Lyotard is therefore worthy of brief examination.

Lyotard is a professor of philosophy who has long been involved in *Socialisme ou Barbarie*. Although he quit the group in 1963 along with those who rejected the unimaginative jumble of ideas with which Castoriadis was seeking to replace Marxism, he now argues that it was only because he found this liquidation insufficiently liquidating. In fact, Lyotard is a particularly opportunistic rat who boasts of having abandoned ship only when it hit the seabed, by which time he had already jumped ship in order to embark on some other wheeze. Be that as it may, he had, like so many other superannuated leftists, been indulging in the various hobbies with which intellectuals occupy their free time—Freudianism, pop art, and avant-garde music—when the spectacular post-1968 *aggiornamento* that spurred every has-been on the scrapheap into action prompted him to try his own luck. Ever cautious, he began by playing the Marxist for Sartre's *Les Temps Modernes*, respectfully discussing Althusser's Stalinist structuralism, just like any old François George would do. But Lyotard realized, well before that amateur recuperator François George ever did, that there was a more meteoric career to be had in the business of cheap and cheerful decomposition. And there he easily outstripped the simplistic ideologues of schizophrenia,[137] who still harp on about unconscious denial, by churning out justifications for the *submissive* unconscious. Henceforth, as a result, Castoriadis is sunk with his technique of pitting his Freudian scraps against what he presents as Marxism, while miring himself in a catch-22 situation by repeating: "It is not that simple."

For Lyotard, on the other hand, everything is very simple: he learned from Freud that human beings, however dispossessed, libidinally invest in their very dispossession in order to come to terms with it. And so, the secret of this social organization is revealed: all activity, or passivity, is libidinal; workers go to work for pleasure; capitalists exploit them for pleasure; Lyotard gets off on cutting-edge cultural consumption and keeps coming back for more.

Thus, what Freud highlighted as the plasticity of human desire, its erosion within and against alienation, its struggles and defeats, is flattened into an acknowledgement of its introvertedness (hence the Möbius strip so beloved by Lyotard as a metaphor for his "libidinal economy")—serving to justify what exists: "Now, therefore, we must completely abandon critique. . . . Let's replace lifeless critique with an attitude closer to what we effectively experience in our current relations with capital, in the office, in the street, in the cinema, on the roads, on holiday, in the museums, hospitals, and bookshops, that is to say a horrified fascination for the entire range of the *machinery* of *delight*."[138] This inventory of the "*machinery* of *delight*" just about sums up the kind of social misery Lyotard thinks is fun, going from office to bookshop. Lyotard may well defend himself against the label of fascist, a label that some backward-looking leftist will always be ready to throw at him, even though he is in fact no more of a fascist than this leftist's Leninism is real. The spectacle has achieved what in fascism had only been embryonic: for example, the "machinery of delight" in its Nuremberg Rally staging is today widely trivialized and diluted in more modern and omnipresent *economical* forms of conditioning, branding, and manipulation. Lyotard is a wannabe who, with ingress into the most sophisticated sector of social conditioning, discovers that it would take a complete moron not to be libidinally fulfilled. Thus Marx (whom this G-rated schoolboy calls "little girl Marx" in the same way that he likes to imagine him jerking off with one hand while writing *Capital* with the other) criticized capitalism in order to defend himself against the fascination it exerted over him. Lyotard is notably defense averse. Multiple forms of the "machinery of delight" (even football matches, although not the concerts of the asinine Buddhist John Cage, which attract only non-events like Cage) frequently serve as the setting and opportunity of rioting and feature crowds of the kind who, like Marx, "defend" themselves in concert with the masses around the world uninterested in happy spectatorship or in Lyotard and his followers' fantasy of "becoming sufficiently anonymous conducting bodies, not in order to stop the effects . . . we have neither to judge causes nor isolate effects, energies pass through us and we have to suffer them."[139] (With prose like that, he'll soon be ripe enough to write blurbs for pop music.)

Lyotard calls the "passivity" he extols "a philosophy of sodomists and women."[140] I leave it to the individuals concerned to respond to the incredible insult of inflicting such a philosophy on them. Note only that the maneuver attempted here of comparing enemies of Lyotard's high-strung vegetable "philosophy" with some "sodomists and women" is particularly crass; it emerges in even more clear-cut fashion in an extraordinary outburst in the form of a question ("From where would you *criticize* fetishism, when you know that one cannot criticize homosexuality or masochism without becoming a crude bastard of the moral order?"[141]), where the social domination of the fetish-character of the commodity is *flatly* identified with the free choice of individual pleasure.

The assiduous gravediggers of theory, critique, and the negative all claim to be working in the name of something far more subversive than these antediluvian Lyotardian clichés, and not simply because they find them of no *interest*. To again quote the unreadable Lyotard (the cruelest thing that could be done to him), there follow some of the dazzling proposals included in his book's closing remarks: "What would be interesting would be to stay put, but quietly seize every chance to function as good intensity-conducting bodies."[142] (Now we can rest reassured that, fresh from his demolition of theory, Lyotard is staying put, not quitting the university to go out on the road, and will carry on for hundreds of pages wondering thus: "Can one think, that is to say distinguish?"[143]) "No need for declarations, manifestos, organizations, provocations, no need for *exemplary actions*."[144] (Absolutely no need for all that in order to work quietly, as any good citizen will tell you.) "Set dissimulation to work on behalf of intensities. Invulnerable conspiracy, headless, homeless, with neither program nor project, deploying a thousand cancerous tensors in the bodies of signs."[145] (Beyond the ridiculous jargon, his conspiracy is as invulnerable as the very reality that escapes existing authority: nobody in their right mind has been waiting for Lyotard to come along in order to resist reification—desire remains.) And to end on a high note: "We invent nothing, that's it, yes, yes, yes, yes."[146] Rather, it is Lyotard who invents nothing, and who then rushes out to patent "libidinal economy"! This closing approbatory trance is, according to him, the "dance" about which he had earlier asked: "Is the *dance* true? One will always be able to say so. But that's not where its force [*puissance*] lies."[147] And so this fan of submissiveness is to Nietzsche what the Folies Bergère dancers are to voodoo.[148] Lyotard's thinking is in fact more car exhaust—at Vincennes—than blue sky: the fumes are his lyricism.

More amusing still owing to the fact that he touches on something a bit less abstract, a Lyotardian Fourierist by the name of Pascal Bruckner ventured to write the following about the arson attack by rioters on the Paris Stock Exchange in May 1968:[149] "One cannot help thinking, however, about what 'Fourierist militants' would have done in the same situation. . . . All the evidence suggests that instead of burning down the building, they would have occupied, cleaned, and lived in it; not for the purpose of turning it into a debating chamber, but in order to transform it in whatever way they wished"[150]—under the benevolent eye of police surveillance, no doubt eager to learn a bit about gastrosophy,[151] and to replace brutal batons and beatings with gourmet disputations. It is nevertheless the case that not one of those people seeking to abolish the negation of life has of course ever negated anything, or ever lived.

When Lyotard wants to describe his *homo libidinous* in greater detail, he instances the scientific researcher who is "an experimenter, indefatigable and not enslaved, with new junctures and combinations of energy,"[152] whom he greatly admires for being not a "subject" but "a small transitory region in a process of incredibly sophisticated energetic metamorphosis."[153] And when he asks himself "what has to be changed?," he dreams of extending this freedom to "*all* the pieces of the social 'body,' without *exception*."[154] Thus this professorial apologist of unemployed knowledge shrugs off his ludicrous pretensions to the point of wanting to exist *without employers*. Similarly, Attali, pointing out where this "exception" lies, deplores the fact that the "most socially volatile" workers are "the least disposed toward the idea of self-management," which "will first affect the top echelons of the managers."[155] (This applies also to the miserable lifestyles portrayed in Guégan's novels, where, under the disintegrating veneer of revolutionist extremism, we find displayed as standard fare the nonchalance and fatuous contentedness typical of today's junior manager—ranging from "shopping for clothes on London's Oxford Street" to the art of lighting a log fire in one's secondary, vacation home.)

In terms of employer and employed, Lyotard, "a small transitory region" in Vincennes, under the aegis of the Stalinist Claude Frioux,[156] is in point of fact the contemporary there of one Michel Meignant, who in turn teaches "the direct, natural, and necessary relation of person to person"[157] under the heading of "sexology." At a time when the last positions of what was once private life have been swept away by the commodity's colonization of everyday life, this relation has in fact taken the form of "the infinite degradation in which man exists for himself."[158] Lyotard, however, now answers even less to his job description. Aiming to address the same misery, he resembles that other product of decadence recently launched in New York: "Several psychoanalysts are responsible for this new craze. To their anxious, traumatized or frustrated patients, they propose the following unexpected 'transference': a simple collar with a leash that the lady has to walk night and day like a real puppy, taking care to observe the traditional stops near streetlamps and car tires. This method of inexpensively filling an emotional void provides as many pretexts for walking as golf" (*France Soir*, April 28, 1973). The thought of Lyotard is a dog of the same kind, a leash with something missing, and is likely to bring as much consolation to those unfortunate enough to have to walk it around the Bois de Vincennes or elsewhere.

Ratgeb

In the course of *A Tale of a Tub*, Jonathan Swift refers to a "curious *Receipt*, a *Nostrum*" that attempts to distil a "universal System in a small portable Volume, of all Things that are to be Known, or Believed, or Imagined, or Practised in Life," and which he then goes on to describe in detail: "You take fair correct Copies, well bound in Calfs Skin, and Lettered at the Back, of all Modern Bodies of Arts and Sciences whatsoever, and in what Language you please. These you distil in balneo Mariae, infusing Quintessence of Poppy Q. S. together with three pints of Lethe, to be had from the Apothecaries. You cleanse away carefully the Sordes and Caput mortuum, letting all that is volatile evaporate. You preserve only the first Running, which is again to be distilled seventeen times," etc., etc.[159]

Recently, a newcomer to the guild of hack anthologists has, thanks to the kind of first-off masterstroke that could lead one to suspect that he might not be as new to the game as he makes out, elevated this type of very specific wordsmithery to a level of technical proficiency fully in keeping with the technical possibilities of the era: he had a computer calculate and produce all the possible and syntactically viable combinations of the seventy-six nouns contained in the table of contents of a decade-old treatise on the revolution of everyday life, a work that had, in its time, been widely regarded as comprehensive.[160] The procedure has an ingenious ring to it, since a large proportion of his target audience only acquires its information by reading contents pages of reputedly important works. The newcomer could thus reasonably expect that his own work, being nothing but a table of contents *many times over*, would therefore be considered important, and perhaps even important to the power of seventy-six.

However, were this possibly a case of a conspiracy hatched by his implacable rivals further dismayed by a work that largely robbed them of festering grist to their collective mill, it would appear not to have met with the success that people were pinning on it. It is not beyond the realm of possibility that its failure may in part be explained by a rumor circulating around the time of this catechism's publication that "Ratgeb" was not the self-managementist flower freshly bloomed from the last dew of the morning after all, but rather a well-trained man of letters who already tried once to raise his public profile by tacking a laborious preface onto a work that could very well have done without it. Here again, he was no doubt relying on the fact that the target audience, the same readers fond of tables of contents, also comprised those who never manage to get beyond the prefaces of most books. In any case, nobody could in all honesty criticize him for the kind of increasingly common, hack prefacer-driven, fairly harmless maneuver with which belle-lettrists everywhere are familiar. What actually raised hackles was the fact that on this occasion he had used the name of a long-dead albeit still highly esteemed author as a pseudonym, thereby apparently seeking to recuperate this esteem for his own advantage.[161] He even went so far as to use the stylistic ornaments that were the hallmark of this author's subtle lyricism, but in an extremely impoverished fashion. Since he later used the same lyricism to put tables of contents onto punch cards, there are some grounds for thinking that he suffers from a chronic case of self-obsession, or perhaps is even undergoing a full-blown identity crisis.

However, to divert attention and conceal his obsessiveness, Ratgeb first announces the key component of his formula for transitioning without further ado "from wildcat strike to generalized self-management": "The following text is an attempt to respond to the problems that will be posed by the transition from a class society to a society of total self-management."[162] Something of a tall order. It is therefore with regard to these problems, as they are posed in reality to the global proletariat, that we must judge his literary prowess. Feeling the overwhelming weight of his inability to address such matters, Ratgeb attempts a self-protective *flanking maneuver* a few lines later, by asserting that the "radicality of his 'notes' is beyond dispute." Emboldened by this initial diktat, he is perfectly willing to concede that his "notes" "deserve to be discussed," only to rule out with immediate effect the participation in this discussion of "intellectual jerks who are only capable of raising abstract objections." Such an authoritarian procedure is no more likely to be followed up by its practical implementation than when the Académie Française says no to the inclusion of the word "creativity" in its dictionary (although the fate of creativity is not sealed as a result, as Ratgeb will be the first to acknowledge). He is not, however, calling for physical violence, that is, concrete criticism *par excellence*. What, then, is not, in his view, abstract criticism? Answer: debate "on the spot, in workplaces whenever anger is mounting." It would indeed take a complete government department or trade union moron not to be able to recognize workplace anger as something well and truly concrete. But if everything else is abstract, Ratgeb himself is simply a more ridiculous abstraction than most, and certainly an "intellectual jerk." There is, after all, no way that he could expect to pass himself off as a worker, angry or otherwise. Nor could he possibly be unaware that whenever he makes a show of using the term "abstract" in the most pedantic way imaginable, he could just as well write the word "worker" fifty thousand times in the course of his pamphlet without the word becoming any more concrete. He cannot in all seriousness even believe that his obsolete prognostications could one day be subject to "on the spot" debate, or even simply be read by revolutionary workers. As he may have gathered from the reception he received in Portugal when he jetted over there with his glad tidings, it is always *too soon* or *too late* for hollow abstractions like his.[163]

On the subject of abstraction and how the abstract conceals itself within the concrete, Ratgeb writes: "Each delegate has the right to resign. It would seem, however, that this right should sometimes be temporarily suspended during the period of self-defense. There is no reason for guerilla volunteers to abandon their comrades in the middle of an armed engagement."[164] Similarly, and leaving guerillas and armed engagements aside for the moment, "there was no reason" for Vaneigem to abandon Paris on May 15, 1968. It is nevertheless clear that such irresponsible desertions will never happen again, now that Ratgeb is around to legislate insurrectionary moments. Yet he can do nothing more for Vaneigem, who seems to have never returned from his untimely holiday.

If Ratgeb's prayer wheel is, like so many others, ultimately nothing more than a *smattering* of ideology, this is attributable only to historical conditions that don't normally favor such applications. This "Zaragoza program" of council communism,[165] as absurd as the earlier one, itself lacks one important detail: the CNT's formal adoption of it. Ratgeb's immaterial extremism spontaneously adopts a ferociously didactic tone in its contempt for reality and those who make it: "Have you ever felt the urge to throw your pay slip back in the face of your employer? In that case, you have come to appreciate that . . ." etc.

(The real question being: has Ratgeb, in the course of his various bits of work on the dregs of B movie French cinema or literary hackwork, ever thrown his pay slip back in anyone's face?) The sycophantic manner he has of banging the drum for self-management is of no use to him whatsoever when it comes to persuading anybody that his muddled outlook has any reality at all, since he at the same time has to assume the bombastically reckless persona of an ideologue in order to posit a clearcut, generally accepted base of agreement concerning every key term—starting with self-management—that he stacks up in demented overkill; terms whose crucially important meanings are at stake in historical struggles, and always hang on their outcome, as anyone with even a scintilla of awareness of twentieth-century revolutionary history would know.

In exchanging his junk for the illusion of being important, Ratgeb chooses to disregard the real problems of modern revolution, the fiction of whose excellence merely serves to try and get people to lap up the minutiae of his specific excellence, his "indisputable" radicality, although nowhere can the practical results of these "qualities" be seen to comply with what he himself stipulates as the test of veracity at the peak of his multilayered, two-faced disingenuousness.

The spirit of generalized self-management is great, and Ratgeb is its prophet. The cascade of his tautologies, coming from and leading nowhere, has swallowed up the real problems of revolution together with its driving force: its history. Where the recent past is concerned, he is a model of discretion and is not bothered about anything more distant. It is thus within his remit to note that Garcia Oliver was not a great supporter of self-management, since he became a government minister,[166] whereupon Ratgeb rains down a few cliché-ridden insults (given his unconscious mannerisms and tics, it is little wonder that the same terms crop up in Ratgeb more than they should). Partisanship and struggles that turn some into government ministers and others into dust on the battlefields of Madrid or Aragon are, understandably, of no concern to Ratgeb. "The Spanish revolutionaries of 1937 condemned themselves to extermination precisely because they had failed to push forward boldly enough and colluded with the reformist and Stalinist rabble."[167] Certainly: it was because it did not succeed that the Spanish Revolution failed. Having learned this valuable lesson from past revolutions, Ratgeb can now tackle the problems of the contemporary era, where he is even more ill at ease since everything remains to be decided. When judged according to Ratgeb's radicalism, Lip workers are branded cowards.[168] (By 1970, Vaneigem was already lambasting the miners of Kiruna for not superseding the Paris Commune.)[169] It is in fact the case that they failed to engineer "a radical break with the commodity system."[170] (It should be added that as much could be expected, since the only way to break with the commodity system is to break it; and obviously it is still in existence, with Ratgeb as a bonus to clamor on about it.) The miners were thus "recuperated from the beginning,"[171] outlawed from all self-managing eternity and as suprahistorical as an initially revolutionary Ratgeb trailing the phantom of his radicality down through the ages.

Ever since scrapings from the Situationist barrel became flavor of the month, there has been no shortage of nonentities to lament the fact that art and philosophy have not been realized within three days of workers rising up to attack the forces exploiting them. It should be said that these nonentities do have a point here, since at the same time, they are ready at any moment to assert that the first strike to come along has no other conscious goal but this very realization. (Otherwise, it would of course be "recuperated from the beginning.") And it is in being regularly disappointed that makes them so harsh. These people would undoubtedly have excoriated the Paris Communards, who, by March 18, 1871, were after all merely patriots who wanted to retain their cannons to wage war on the Germans. But it must be said that such impudent stupidity is a very modern phenomenon, and that it will of course always be happy to step in and shed its own light wherever history has already made everything clear. What these gentlemen lack, apart from the dialectic, which no one demands of them, is a modicum of decency in their imbecility.

To return to our subject, Ratgeb shouts loudly and repeatedly "to arms!," proudly rattling his bladeless, gripless saber, pompously declaring that "saber-rattling marks the happiest day of my life."[172] But he no longer believes in his own hollow rantings, or even in their success with any audience: he runs on momentum alone. All those who speak of self-management and workers' councils, or even about (you must be joking) transparency and subversive play without referring explicitly to the concrete conditions of contemporary class struggle, and to the possibilities and necessities they contain— such people have a corpse in their mouth: the corpse of the Situationist International. Some bitterly chew things over while others choke. Ratgeb is simply the most *apoplectic* one among them (apoplexy: the sudden and more or less complete cessation of brain function, accompanied by loss of consciousness and voluntary movement, without any suspension of respiration and blood circulation).

ENOUGH!

The confusionism of recuperation had its heyday at a historical juncture that is now ending, where the movement of subversion that spread throughout society after 1968 was still realizing praxis on a new, considerably enlarged and qualitatively advanced basis, albeit well below the level of general and, in particular, theoretical development attained in the previous moment by more narrowly based revolutionary activity, through the Situationist International. Recuperators have thrived on this apparent mismatch and die off from what is abolished by the advance of revolutionary reality, where the needs of the new era independently discover, beyond the screen of delusory conceptions that cannot be translated into forces (and barely into words), the specific tasks and deeds which contemporary revolutionary struggle must appropriate and bear out, and will supersede. I cannot therefore be credited with the annihilation of the recuperators: their noisy non-existence dissipates by itself (as evidenced in the case of the twilight years of *Actuel*, that garbage dump of recuperation), with a murmur already lost in the cacophony of a decaying spectacle. Over this collection of vermin I have done no more than lay the tombstone, and hereby engrave upon it what shall perforce remain their epitaph:

Fama di loro il mondo non lassa misericordia e giustizia gli sdegna: non ragioniam di lor, ma guarda e passa.

[Fame of them the world hath none, Nor suffers; mercy and justice scorn them both.

Speak not of them, but look, and pass them by.]

—Dante's *Inferno*

Notes

Preface

1. Semprún is here anticipating the various concepts found in the thinkers of the dictionary to follow. *Libidinal Economy* is a 1974 book by French philosopher Jean-François Lyotard, while "desiring machines" (*machines désirantes*) is a term coined by Gilles Deleuze and Félix Guattari in their 1972 *Anti-Oedipus*.

2. This sentence is an appropriation of a line from one of Comte de Lautréamont's poems (*Poésies* I.18), in which it is said that a good appreciation of Voltaire's works is preferable to the works themselves.

3. Semprún is referring to the Carnation Revolution in Portugal which began on April 25, 1974, with a military coup in Lisbon that toppled the Salazar dictatorship. The coup was coupled with grassroots social resistance involving workers and peasants, which turned the events into a popular revolution. In May the following year, Semprún published *La Guerre Sociale au Portugal* with Éditions Champ Libre, which examined the first year of the events.

4. "I would display too much honor to my subject were I to treat it in an orderly fashion. I want to show that it is unworthy of such a treatment." Guy Debord, *Considerations on the Assassination of Gérard Lebovici*, trans. Robert Greene (London: TamTam Books, 2001), 3.

Recuperation in France since 1968

1. Starting already in the 1890s, perhaps with the work of Eduard Bernstein, up until Antonio Negri's 1979 *Marx Beyond Marx*, but also thereafter, there have been innumerable studies seeking to expunge from the work of Marx elements deemed dated or simply inaccurate, and therein provide corrective developments to his work.

2. The Situationist International dissolved itself in 1972. For an autobiography of its twilight, see Situationist International, "Theses of the Situationist

International and Its Time," in *The Real Split in the International*, trans. John McHale (London: Pluto Press, 2003).

3. Otelo Nuno Romão Saraiva de Carvalho was a Portuguese military officer and chief strategist of the 1974 Carnation Revolution. He assumed leadership roles in the first Portuguese Provisional Governments.

4. Jean Cardonnel was a leftist Catholic and the main proponent of liberation theology in France.

5. Jean-François Lyotard, *Libidinal Economy* (1974), trans. Iain Hamilton Grant (Indianapolis: Indiana University Press, 1993), 262.

6. PCF is the acronym for the French Communist Party, while Socialisme ou Barbarie was a left communist, council communist, and anarchist group operating out of France during the postwar period (1949–1967). Its members included Cornelius Castoriadis and Jean-François Lyotard, both of whom appear among the entries here.

7. Claude Lefort was a French political philosopher and founding member of the Socialisme ou Barbarie group along with Castoriadis. Lefort was a frequent contributor to *Les Temps Modernes* and studied under phenomenologist Maurice Merleau-Ponty.

8. Ratgeb, who also receives an entry in the dictionary to follow, is the pseudonym of Raoul Vaneigem, prominent member of the Situationist International and author of *The Revolution of Everyday Life* (*Traité de savoir-vivre à l'usage des jeunes générations*, 1967). Vaneigem resigned from the SI in 1970. Soon after, the SI issued a critical response. See Situationist International, "Appendix 5: Communiqué from the SI concerning Vaneigem," in *The Real Split in the International: Theses on the Situationist International and Its Time*, trans. John McHale (London: Pluto Press, 2003), 145–168.

9. Bernard Buffet was a French expressionist painter and member of the anti-abstract art group L'homme Témoin. Georges Mathieu was a French abstract painter and member of the Académie des Beaux-Arts in Paris.

10. Henri Lefebvre was a French Marxist philosopher and sociologist, best known for pioneering the critique of everyday life and for his critical engagement the concept of urbanism, most notably in *The Production of Space* (1974).

11. The term "dramaturgical society [*société théâtrale*]" gained a certain prominence for sociological studies in France and the United States during the 1960s. Here it is posited that on the stage, as in life, social relationships are supported by a set of conventions that constitute a universe of theatricality. See Erving Goffman, *The Presentation of the Self in Everyday Life* (New York: Doubleday, 1959), or, more recently, Emmanuelle Cabin Saint Marcel, "Une société théâtrale ou théâtralisée? La vision des sociologues français et américains depuis 1967," *Sciences de l'Homme et Société*, 2013.

12. The terms "discourses of power" and the "tyranny of discourse" allude to the genealogical work of Michel Foucault, who Semprún also includes as an entry below. However, the references here are more general in their implication toward poststructuralism and perhaps, more recently, bear a pertinence for standpoint epistemology.

13. Comte de Lautréamont, *Maldoror and Poems* (London: Penguin Classics, 1978), §2.

14. Ivan Illich was a Roman Catholic priest, theologian, philosopher, and social critic. Maurice Clavel was a French writer, journalist, and philosopher. The latter was politicized during the May 1968 upheaval in France. The Taizé community is an ecumenical monastic order, with a strong devotion to peace and justice through prayer and meditation, based in in Taizé, Saône-et-Loire, Burgundy. It has become one of the world's most popular sites of Christian youth pilgrimage.

15. Philippe Sollers is a French writer and critic, and founder of the literary journal *Tel Quel*.

16. Cf. the US underground comix movement (1967–1979), whose most famous cartoonist is Robert Crumb.

17. René Viénet is a sinologist, French filmmaker, and former member of the Situationist International. Most notably in *Can Dialectics Break Bricks?* (1973), Viénet used the situationist technique of *détournement*: a collage-like approach to cultural objects whereby pre-existing elements are reassembled and rearranged towards new subversive purposes. In the film, Viénet appropriates the 1972 martial arts film *Crush* by Tu Guangqi, whose heroic plot focuses on an anti-colonialist revolt in Korea during the period of Japanese occupation. Viénet replaces all of the dialogue with his own subtitles, transforming the story into one of class conflict and parliamentary and Leninist betrayal of the proletariat, against the backdrop of kung fu fighting. *Détournement* involved a quotation or aesthetic element reused or adapted to ends other than its initial intention and within an entirely new context. It both transcends the bourgeois cult of originality and the private ownership of thought. See Guy Debord and Gil J. Wolman, "A User's Guide to Détournement," in *Situationist International Anthology*, rev. and exp. ed., trans. Ken Knabb (Berkeley: Bureau of Public Secrets, 2006), 14–21.

18. Maximilien Rubel was a Marxist historian and council communist, born in the Ukraine but emigrated to France and lived under the German occupation. The "exhaustion" referred to here is likely in reference to Rubel's immense intellectual output.

19. Amadeo Bordiga was an Italian Marxist and communist theorist, founder of the Communist Party of Italy, and leading figure of the International Communist Party. He is one of the most notable representatives of left communism in Europe.

20. The reference here is to a collection of writings from *L'Ennemi du peuple*, an anarchist journal from the early twentieth century on which Darien collaborated. The volume was published by Éditions Champ Libre in 1972, with Guégan providing minimal commentary.

21. Lyotard, *Libidinal Economy*, 66; translation amended.

22. This quotation comes from Semprún's own 1975 *La Guerre sociale au Portugal* (Paris: Éditions Champ Libre), 46.

Small Dictionary of the Great Names of Recuperation

1. Originally *le Désagrégé-de-Philosophie*; the French pun is lost here in the translation. The corollary *agrégé* refers to the title of university teachers in France, after having passed the *agrégation*, a competitive examination for civil service in the French educational system. Semprún's nomenclature for Franklin as *le Désagrégé-de-Philosophie* thereby suggests both intellectual folly and professional failure.

2. Jacques Attali, *La parole et l'outil* (Paris: Presses Universitaires de France, 1975), 156–157.

3. Joseph Stalin, "Address to the Graduates from the Red Army Academies" (Delivered in the Kremlin, 4 May 1935).

4. Attali, *La parole et l'outil*, 155.

5. Attali, 154.

6. Étienne Cabet and Charles Fourier were both French utopian socialists of the late eighteenth and early nineteenth centuries.

7. Attali, *La parole et l'outil*, 174.

8. Atali, 86–87.

9. Atali, 200.

10. Edgar Morin is a French philosopher and sociologist of media studies and theories of information. He was a founder and director of the journal *Arguments* (1954–1962).

11. Attali, *La parole et l'outil*, 120.

12. Attali, 120.

13. Attali, 15.

14. Pierre Larousse was a nineteenth-century French grammarian, lexicographer, and encyclopedist. He founded Éditions Larousse, a French publishing house specializing in dictionaries. Its best-known work is the *Petit Larousse*, a 1905 French-language encyclopedic dictionary.

15. Internationale situationniste, "Comment on ne comprend pas des livres situationnistes," in *Internationale situationniste: Édition augmentée* (Paris: Librairie Arthème Fayard, 1997), 621.

16. Attali, *La parole et l'outil*, 241.

17. Attali, 177.

18. Again, there are puns here in the original French difficult to render in English. *L'erre nouvelle* sounds strikingly similar to *l'ère nouvelle* or "new era," while *le champ du signe* homophonically alludes to *le chant du cygne* or "swan song."

19. Jacques Attali and Marc Guillaume, *L'anti-économique* (Paris: Presses Universitaires de France, 1974), 25.

20. A *coquille* is a typographic error, which adds a pun to this description of a technique of falsification.

21. *Maspérisé*, a neologism referring to François Maspero and his publishing house Éditions Maspero. The Situationists coined the term "to masperize" to describe the butchering, falsification, or corruption of a text, for instance by deleting segments from a quote without marking them (cf. Guy Debord, *Correspondance*, vol. 3: *Janvier 1965–Décembre 1968* [Paris: Librairie Arthème Fayard, 2003], 293). Maspero owned the bookstore La Joie de Lire on rue Saint Severin for nearly twenty years, itself a militant hub for *tiers-mondiste* activism. Éditions Maspero first published Franz Fanon's *Wretched of the Earth* with its preface by Sartre, as well as works by Ben Barka, Che Guevara, Malcolm X, and others.

22. Coauthor of *L'anti-économique* with Attali, Marc Guillaume is a French economist who, along with Attali, campaigned for Mitterrand.

23. Régis Debray is a French philosopher of media and journalist who became an official advisor on Foreign Affairs to Mitterrand after the 1981 presidential elections, as well as an advisor to Salvador Allende. See T. J. Clark and Donald Nicholson-Smith, "Why Art Can't Kill the Situationist International," *October* 79 (Winter 1997).

24. Jean Barrot is a pseudonym for Gilles Dauvé. He and François Martin (penname of François Cerruti) wrote *Eclipse and Re-Emergence of the Communist Movement*, a collection of essays written between 1969 and 1972 that deal with a variety of issues around the refusal of work, revolution, and the legacy of left communism and the ultra-left.

25. Gilles Dauvé and François Martin, "Foreword to the 1974 Black & Red Edition," in *Eclipse and Re-emergence of the Communist Movement* (Oakland: PM Press, 2015), 15.

26. Jean-Yves Bériou, "Théorie révolutionnaire et cycles historiques," postface to Ferdinand Domela Nieuwenhuis, *Le socialisme en danger* (Paris: Payot, 1975).

27. Bériou, "Théorie révolutionnaire," 43.

28. Bériou, 39.

29. Internationale situationniste, "A propos de Nantes," *Internationale situationniste: Édition augmentée* (Paris: Librairie Arthème Fayard, 1997), 669.

30. Émile Marenssin, *La 'Bande à Baader' ou La violence révolutionnaire* (Paris: Champ Libre, 1972).

31. The reference here is to *Sans Patrie Ni Frontières* (*Out of the Night*) by Jan Valtin (pseudonym of Richard Julius Hermann Krebs), an expurgated translation from the English by Jean-Claude Henriot, afterword by Jacques Baynac (Paris: Éditions Jean-Claude Lattès, 1975). The *unexpurgated* version of this French translation by Henriot had been published in 1947 by Éditions Dominique Wapler (Paris: Éditions de la Maison Française-New York). Baynac also wrote the preface for *La Bande à Baader ou, la violence révolutionnaire* (Paris: Éditions Champ Libre, 1972), under the pseudonym Émile Marenssin.

32. Attali, *La parole et l'outil*, 6.

33. Internationale situationniste, "Socialisme ou Planète," in *Internationale situationniste: Édition augmentée* (Paris: Librairie Arthème Fayard, 1997), 489–491.

34. Cornelius Castoriadis, "On the History of the Workers' Movement," *telos* no. 30 (1976): 8.

35. Castoriadis, "On the History of the Workers' Movement," 38–39; translation amended.

36. Castoriadis, 4.

37. G. W. F. Hegel, *Phenomenology of Spirit*, trans. A. V. Miller (Oxford: Oxford University Press, 1977), 47.

38. Karl Marx, "The Holy Family," in *Marx and Engels Collected Works*, vol. 4 (London: Progress Publishers, 1975), 37.

39. Castoriadis, "On the History of the Workers' Movement," 4; translation amended.

40. Castoriadis, 4; translation amended.

41. While in London, Marx came to be known as the "Red Terror Doctor."

42. Castoriadis, "On the History of the Workers' Movement," 5; translation amended.

43. Castoriadis, 5; translation amended.

44. Castoriadis, 5; translation amended.

45. Castoriadis, 24; translation amended.

46. Paraphrase of *Timothy 2*, ch. 2, v. 19.

47. Castoriadis, "On the History of the Workers' Movement," 27; translation amended.

48. Castoriadis, 27–28; translation amended.

49. Situationist International, "The Beginning of an Era," in *Situationist International Anthology*, 294.

50. Castoriadis, "On the History of the Workers' Movement," 40–41.

51. Castoriadis, 42.

52. Castoriadis, 39.

53. Castoriadis, 41.

54. Castoriadis, 14.

55. Marx, "The Holy Family," 36.

56. Castoriadis, "On the History of the Workers' Movement," 12; translation amended.

57. Castoriadis, 18, 19, 21; translation amended.

58. This reference is to Jacques Gautrat, who wrote a series of narratives about his experience as a machinist in the French automobile industry at Renault's Billancourt factory for Socialisme ou Barbarie, under the pseudonym Daniel Mothé. Mothé was the gratuitous "worker" in the group who would go on to join the CFDT and publish material in *Arguments* and *L'Express* (see Stephen Hastings-King, *Looking for the Proletariat: Socialisme ou Barbarie and the Problem of Worker Writing* [Leiden: Brill, 2014]).

59. Cornelius Castoriadis, *The Imaginary Institution of Society: Creativity and Autonomy in the Social-Historical World*, trans. Kathleen Blamey (Cambridge: Polity, 1997).

60. Alain Guillerm and Yvon Bourdet, *L'Autogestion* (Paris: Seghers, 1975).

61. Pierre François Lacenaire was a nineteenth-century outlaw and poet. In *Discipline and Punish*, Foucault describes Lacenaire as a new kind of publicly romanticized delinquent. Michel Foucault, *Discipline and Punish: The Birth of the Prison*, trans. Alan Sheridan (New York: Vintage Books, 1995), 283–290.

62. This terrain of mixed woodland and pasture acquired particular significance in the Chouannerie during the French Revolution. It was also significant during the Battle of Normandy in World War II.

63. Foucault, *Discipline and Punish*, 284; translation amended.

64. Marcel Duchamp, "Abridged Dictionary of Surrealism" (1938), in *Salt Seller: The Writings of Marcel Duchamp*, ed. Michel Sanouillet and Elmer Peterson (New York: Oxford University Press, 1973), 107.

65. Situationist International, "Cinema and Revolution," in *Situationist International Anthology*, 378–379.

66. Foucault, *Discipline and Punish*, 284.

67. Foucault, 283.

68. Foucault, 283.

69. Theodor Reik was a psychoanalyst who was trained as one of Freud's first students in Vienna, and a pioneer of lay analysis in the United States. His first major book, *The Compulsion to Confess* (1925), argued that neurotic symptoms such as blushing and stuttering could be seen as unconscious confessions that express the patient's repressed impulses. Reik further explored this theme in *The Unknown Murderer* (1932), where he examined the process of psychologically profiling unknown criminals. He argued that because of unconscious guilt, criminals often leave clues that can lead to their identification and arrest.

70. Pierre François Lacenaire, *The Memoirs of Lacenaire*, trans. Philip John Stead (New York: Roy Publishers, 1955), 158.

71. Lacenaire, *Memoirs*, 36.

72. Lacenaire, 154.

73. Cause Commune Collective, *Le Pourrissement des Sociétés*, 1975.

74. Cause Commune Collective, *Revue d'Esthétique: Présences d'Adorno*, 1975.

75. *10/18* (Union générale d'éditions, UGE) is a French publishing house belonging to the Editis group, founded in 1962 by Paul Chantrel (general manager of Éditions Plon) and publishing paperback formats (books measuring approximately 10×18 cm, hence the name). Éditions 10/18 offered philosophical works, history, and French fiction, publishing in particular works of the Nouveau Roman movement. Jean Duvignaud was a French novelist, sociologist, anthropologist, and former editor for *Arguments*.

76. Pierre Souvestre and Marcel Allain were French writers of the early twentieth century, most remembered for creating the fictional arch-villain and master criminal Fantômas, a popular character in the history of French crime fiction.

77. Vincennes here and throughout the present work refers to Université Paris 8 Vincennes-Saint-Denis. The Château de Cerisy-la-Salle, located in the French commune of Cerisy-la-Salle, hosts the Centre culturel international de Cerisy-la-Salle, a venue for intellectual and scholarly encounters founded in 1952 by Anne Heurgon-Desjardins. The center is the home of the famous "Colloques de Cerisy," a series of seminars renowned in the history of French intellectual life.

78. Although referring to the fact that Jean Franklin is a pseudonym for François George, here Semprún alludes to his brother, Jean-Pierre George, who was mistakenly thought to be the true identity of Jean-Patrick Manchette, a novelist of crime fiction. The line itself is an appropriation from Fontaine's rendition of Aesop's fable "The Wolf and the Lamb."

79. Jean Franklin, *Le discours du pouvoir* (Paris: Éditions 10/18, 1975), back-cover blurb.

80. The original phrase "les mots *travaillent*" comes from the essay "All the King's Men," *Internationale Situationniste*, no. 8 (1963): "The problem of language is at the heart of all the struggles between the forces striving to abolish the present alienation and those striving to maintain it. It is inseparable from the very terrain of those struggles. We live within language as within polluted air. Despite what humorists think, words do not play. Nor do they make love, as Breton thought, except in dreams. Words *work*—on behalf of the dominant organization of life." Situationist International, "All the King's Men," in *Situationist International Anthology*, 149.

81. Joseph Gabel's *False Consciousness: An Essay on Reification* (1962) synthesizes Marxist notions of false consciousness and reification with the study of schizophrenia. Through a synthesis of Georg Lukács's theory of reification, Karl Mannheim's concept of total ideology, and the interwar existential and phenomenological psychiatry of Eugène Minkowski and Ludwig Binswanger, Gabel provides a psycho-sociological theory of consciousness in accordance with dialectical thought, specifically through a parallel between a reified relation to the world and a clinical psychiatric condition of schizophrenia, both sharing a rationality that subordinates temporal experience to excessive spatialization. Here, reification is said to be analogous to the pathologies of schizophrenia.

82. Franklin, *Le discours du pouvoir*, 215, 214, and 220.

83. A reference to the Battle of Austerlitz (2 December 1805), one of the most important and decisive engagements of the Napoleonic Wars. In what is widely regarded as the greatest victory achieved by Napoleon I, the Grande Armée of France defeated the larger Russo-Austrian armies. Semprún is here satirically casting Franklin as Napoleon addressing Baudrillard.

84. Franklin, *Le discours du pouvoir*, 314–315.

85. This expression for a complicated or unpleasant situation refers to the rout of Napoleon's army in 1812. Napoleon led his troops against the Russians in Moscow, an error on the part of the emperor, who found himself blocked in front of the river Berezina, which was impassable. His army suffered heavy losses due to cold and starvation.

86. Kristin Ross, "Lefebvre on the Situationists: An Interview," *October* 79 (1997): 69.

87. Franklin, *Le discours du pouvoir*, 416.

88. Franklin, 412.

89. Franklin, 223.

90. Jean-François Lyotard, *Des dispositifs pulsionnels* (Paris: Galilée, 1994), 222.

91. Franklin, *Le discours du pouvoir*, 201.

92. For an analysis of the *pro-situ* phenomenon, see Situationist International, *The Real Split in the International: Theses on the Situationist International and Its Time*, trans. John McHale (London: Pluto Press, 2003).

93. Franklin, *Le discours du pouvoir*, 412.

94. Jean Franklin was indeed a pseudonym for François George, unmasked here by Semprún.

95. Jean Elleinstein was a French historian and kremlinologist who, between 1972 and 1975, published a four-volume history of the USSR, authorized by the PCF during the Union of the Left.

96. Aleksandr Solzhenitsyn was a political prisoner and Soviet dissident who helped raise global awareness of political repression in the Soviet Union, in particular the Gulag system with the 1973 publication of *The Gulag Archipelago*.

97. André Glucksmann, *La cuisinière et le mangeur d'hommes: Essai sur l'État, le marxisme, les camps de concentration* (Paris: Éditions du Seuil, 1975).

98. André Glucksmann, *La cuisinière*, 9.

99. The town of Vorkuta is associated with Vorkutlag, one of the most notorious forced-labour camps of the Gulag.

100. Glucksmann, *La cuisinière*, 9–10. The wax museum referred to here is the Musée Grévin in Paris.

101. Maurice Merleau-Ponty and Jean-Paul Sartre, "Les jours de notre vie," *Les Temps modernes* 51 (January 1950): 1153–1168.

102. Bernard-Henri Lévy, *Le Nouvel Observateur*, June 30, 1975. The six titles Lévy lists are Guy Lardreau, "Le Singe d'or: Essai sur le concept d'étape du marxisme," in *Essais Mercure De France* (Paris: Mercure De France, 1973); Guy Hocquenghem, *L'après-mai des faunes: Préface de Gilles Deleuze* (Paris: Grasset, 1974); François Fourquet, ed., "Généalogie du capital 2. L'idéal historique," *Recherches*, no. 14 (1974); Jean-Paul Dollé, *Le Désir de révolution* (Paris: Grasset, 1972); Jean-Paul Dollé, *Voie d'accès au plaisir: La métaphysique* (Paris: Grasset, 1974); Jacques Rancière, *Althusser's Lesson* (1975), trans. Emiliano Battista (London: Bloomsbury, 2011).

103. Jean Daniel Bensaid was a French journalist, founder, and executive editor of *Le Nouvel Observateur*. The reference to Mário Soares—first secretary general of the Socialist Party in Portugal from its foundation in 1973 to 1986, and prime minister from 1976 to 1978 and from 1983 to 1985—is to Bensaid's praise over the politician during the Carnation Revolution of 1974.

104. An appropriation of a line from Hegel's *Phenomenology of Spirit*: "Absolute as the night in which, as the saying goes, all cows are black—this is cognition naively reduced to vacuity" (9).

105. The Gauche prolétarienne was a French Maoist group from 1968 to 1974, forming after a split in the Union des jeunesses communistes marxistes-léninistes (UJC-ML), whose members included many that would become leading mouthpieces of Nouvelle Philosophie, including Glucksmann and Bernard-Henri Lévy.

106. Pierre Georges Daix was a French journalist and biographer of Louis Aragon: *Aragon: Une vie à changer* (Paris: Éditions du Seuil, 1975).

107. Alain Jouffroy was a French writer, poet, artist, and friend of Louis Aragon. The quoted formulations are from the concluding comments of his preface to a collection of poems by André Breton, *Clair de terre* (Paris: Éditions Gallimard, 1966).

108. CGT stands for the Confédération Générale du travail, the second largest confederation of trade unions in France, after the CFDT.

109. A notable episode that took place on May 8, 1968, provided by Cohn-Bendit, is worth recalling:

> As the students stood talking they were joined by scores of passers-by, among them Louis Aragon, that venerable bard and prophet of the Communist Party, the man who had sung paeans of praise to OGPU and Stalinism, and who had come to take his place among those who "remind

me so movingly of my own youth." A group of students recognized him and greeted him with cries of "Long live OGPU! Long live Stalin, the father of all the people!" . . . The young demonstrators . . . would have no truck with members of a party whose official organ, *L'Humanité*, had launched what could only be called a smear campaign against French youth. The revolutionary movement did not deny the importance, and even the necessity, of a dialogue with the rank and file of the Communist Party, but it did try to unmask the opportunist strategy and counter-revolutionary attitude of its leaders, including Louis Aragon, the poet laureate of the personality cult. He could not make himself heard simply because those participating in the "teach-out" knew that he had nothing in common with them. His bold assertion that he was in the Party "precisely because he was on the side of youth" merely turned him into a laughingstock. By refusing to act honestly for once in his life, and to denounce the machinations of his Party, he threw away his chance to join the student movement, and incidentally saved his leaders a great deal of embarrassment. [Daniel Cohn-Bendit and Gabriel Cohn-Bendit, *Obsolete Communism: The Left-Wing Alternative*, trans. Arnold Pomerans [London: AK Press, 1992], 58)

110. Alain Jouffrey, "Introduction au mouvement perpétuel d'Aragon," in *Le mouvement perpétuel* (Paris: Gallimard, 1970).

111. Mont Valérien, west of Paris, was a primary location of the execution of resistance fighters and hostages in France by the German army during World War II. In 1960, a memorial was built to honor the resistance fighters and deportees. On June 18, 1971, Maurice Clavel and others associated with the Maoist group Gauche prolétarienne visited the memorial to lay a wreath for the victims of fascism.

112. Glucksmann, *La cuisinière*, 40.

113. "Bleating [*bêlant*]" is a reference to the anarcho hippie communities of the 1970s, where raising sheep in Larzac became a popular lifestyle. The Fight for the Larzac was a civil disobedience campaign by farmers resisting the extension of an existing military base on the Larzac plateau in Southwestern France. The action lasted from 1971 to 1981 and ended in victory when newly elected President Mitterrand formally abandoned the project (see Kristin Ross, *May '68 and Its Afterlives* [Chicago: University of Chicago Press, 2002], 121).

114. *Le Figaro* is one of the largest and oldest national dailies in France and renowned for its right-wing editorial line.

115. Andrei Sakharov was a Soviet nuclear physicist and dissident who was awarded the Nobel Peace Prize in 1975 for his opposition to the abuse of power and his work supporting human rights.

116. Michel Lancelot was a French television journalist and radio host.

117. Michel Lancelot, *Le jeune lion dort avec ses dents: Genies et faussaires de la contre-culture* (Paris: Albin Michel, 1974).

118. Jean-François Revel was a center-left editor and journalist at *L'Express* who in the mid-1960s was considered part of Mitterrand's inner circle. Revel later became a prominent European proponent of classical liberalism and free market economics.

119. Jean-Louis "Bulldog" Brau was an early member of the Lettrist International.

120. Lancelot, *Le jeune lion dort avec ses dents*, 184–186.

121. The Kiruna mine of the Lapland in Sweden is the largest and most modern underground iron ore mine in the world. On December 9, 1969, a miners' strike erupted in the ore fields of Norrbotten in northern Sweden. It was a wildcat strike in which 4,800 miners at LKAB's (Loussavaara-Kiirunavaara AB) mines in Svappavaara, Kiruna, and Malmberget halted work for 57 days.

122. This is a reference to part of Balzac's *La Comédie humaine*, "Scenes from Parisian life."

123. Pierre Alexis Ponson du Terrail was a nineteenth-century French writer and prolific novelist, producing in the space of twenty years about seventy-three volumes.

124. François Bott is a French author and journalist who had his own column in *Le Monde*, which gave a glowing write-up of Guégan's second novel, *Les Irréguliers*: François Bott, "Gérard Guégan et ses 'Irréguliers,'" *Le Monde*, February 28, 1975. In the same issue, Guégan published "Conjuguer le présent."

125. Gérard Guégan, "Conjuguer le present," *Le Monde*, February 28, 1975.

126. Guégan, "Conjuguer le present."

127. Gérard Guégan, *La rage au cœur* (Paris: Éditions Champ Libre, 1974).

128. A lifelong member of the PCF, André Stil was a French novelist and political activist. In November 1956, he was *L'Humanité*'s special envoy to Budapest during the Soviet Union's response to the Hungarian uprising and, as an ardent supporter of the latter, wrote an editorial entitled "Budapest Smiles." Guégan appeared in the TV film *La Croisée* (1975), directed by Raoul Sangla, with a screenplay by Stil.

129. The film producer and founder of Éditions Champ Libre, Gérard Lebovici fired four employees including Guégan on November 4, 1974 (see Éditions Champ Libre, *Correspondance*, vol. 1 [Paris: Éditions Champ Libre, 1978]).

130. Ernest Cœurderoy was a nineteenth-century medical doctor, revolutionary journalist, libertarian writer, and participant in the 1848 Revolution in France.

He lived in exile for most of his life. Vaneigem wrote a preface to a collection of writings Cœurderoy entitled "Terrorism or Revolution" published by Éditions Champ Libre in 1972. "Éditions Champ Libre have of course just published Vaneigem's short, absolutely appalling preface to a selection of Ernest Cœurderoy's writings. Vaneigem has again assumed the *pro-situ* mantle. He points out that 'the Situationist project' still has his approval but that as far as the SI is concerned, his attitude to it since November 1970 has merely been one of 'indifference'! Written from a quite clearly *decomposed* theoretical perspective, his preface is a full-blown *pastiche* of his own former style, a preface whose very existence is enough to make him look ridiculous" (Guy Debord, *Correspondance*, vol. 4: *Janvier 1969–Décembre 1972* [Paris: Librairie Arthème Fayard, 2004], 519).

131. Gérard Guégan, *Les Irréguliers* (Paris: J.C. Lattès, 1975), 244.

132. Nick Quarry, *The Vendetta* (New York: Gold Medal Books, 1963), trans. By Suzanne Sinet as *Le Cri du Sang* (Paris: Gallimard, série noire, 1975); Jean-Patrick Manchette, *Nada* (1972), trans. Donald-Nicholson Smith (New York: New York Review of Books, 2019).

133. *Actuel* (1967–1994) was a French magazine that started out covering avant-garde jazz and alternative music but, after 1970, became a periodical echoing post-1968 libertarian sentiments.

134. Jean François Paul de Gondi de Retz, *Memoirs of the Cardinal de Retz*, vol. 2, trans. Peter Davall (London: T. Becket, T. Cadell, and T. Evans, 1723), 214.

135. William Burroughs and Brion Gysin, *The Electronic Revolution* (Cambridge: Blackmore Head Press, 1971); *Révolution Électronique: Suivi de Time et de Étoile Morte*, trans. Jean Chopin (Paris: Éditions Champ Libre, 1974).

136. Guégan wrote *Napoléon, Comment faire la guerre* (1973) under the pseudonym Yann Cloarec. He then wrote *Les Rejetés* (1974) under the pseudonym Yves Le Braz.

137. Namely, Gilles Deleuze and Félix Guattari.

138. Lyotard, *Libidinal Economy*, 140; translation amended. Although Grant retains the French in "*dispositifs* of *jouissance*," "*machinery* of *delight*" works better for Semprún's intervention, particularly in relation to Leni Riefenstahl's Nazi propaganda film, *Triumph of the Will*, to which Semprún is clearly referring.

139. Lyotard, *Libidinal Economy*, 258.

140. Lyotard, 258.

141. Lyotard, 110.

142. Lyotard, 262.

143. Lyotard, 170.

144. Lyotard, 262.

145. Lyotard, 262.

146. Lyotard, 262.

147. Lyotard, 262.

148. The Folies Bergère is a Parisian cabaret music hall opened in the second half of the nineteenth century. In the early twentieth century, performances featured extravagant costumes, sets, and effects, and often nude dancing.

149. On May 24, 1968, the former Paris Stock Exchange building, the Bourse des Valeurs, was set on fire in the midst of country-wide wildcat strikes, occupations, and conflicts with police.

150. Pascal Bruckner, *Fourier* (Paris: Seuil, 1975). Bruckner is a French writer, one of the nouveaux philosophes that came to prominence in the late 1970s.

151. From the French *la gastrosophie*, a Fourierist concept that combines gastronomy and philosophy.

152. Lyotard, *Libidinal Economy*, 254.

153. Lyotard, 253; translation amended.

154. Lyotard, 254.

155. Attali, *La parole et l'outil*, 166.

156. Claude Frioux was a French academic specializing in Russia and became professor emeritus at the Université Paris 8 (Centre Universitaire Expérimental de Vincennes).

157. Karl Marx, "Economic and Philosophic Manuscripts of 1844," in *Marx and Engels Collected Works*, vol. 3 (London: Progress Publishers, 1975), 295. Michel Meignant is a therapeutic psychologist specializing in sexology and, more recently, "loveology." He taught analytic humanist sexology at the Université Paris 8 from 1974 to 1980.

158. Marx, "Economic and Philosophic Manuscripts of 1844," 295.

159. Jonathan Swift, "A Tale of a Tub," in *The Writings of Jonathan Swift* (New York: Norton Critical Editions, 1973), 327–328.

160. Raoul Vaneigem, *The Revolution of Everyday Life* (1967), trans. Donald Nicholson-Smith (Oakland, CA: PM Press, 2012).

161. Without mentioning Raoul Vaneigem's name, Semprún reverses name usage, inferring for satirical purposes that "Ratgeb" once used Vaneigem's name as a pseudonym.

162. Raoul Vaneigem, *From Wildcat Strike to Total Self-Management* (1974), trans. Paul Sharkey and Ken Knabb (Berkeley: Bureau of Public Secrets, 2001), 7; translation amended.

163. During the Carnation Revolution, Vaneigem traveled to Portugal in the spring of 1974 for a few days to anonymously distribute a pamphlet on proletarian self-management. In a May 1974 letter to Eduardo Rothe, Guy Debord gives his judgment: "I heard that the risible Vaneigem has run off not to Lisbon but to Porto—provincialism obligates! It is there to be found the only *two* supporters he has in the world; they who were denounced as part-time cops over two years ago by the others in Lisbon. I do not think, however, that the struggle against Vaneigemism is a job for Portuguese revolutionaries. Vaneigem would break for the border if he ever happened to come across one" (Guy Debord, *Correspondance*, vol. 5: *Janvier 1973–Décembre 1978* [Paris: Libraire Arthème Fayard, 2005], 159).

164. Vaneigem, *From Wildcat Strike to Total Self-Management*, 59; translation amended.

165. A reference to the May 1936 Congress of the *Confederación Nacional del Trabajo* (CNT) held in Saragossa.

166. Joan Garcia Oliver was an anarcho-syndicalist who in 1936 became minister of justice in the Second Spanish Republic.

167. Vaneigem, *From Wildcat Strike to Total Self-Management*, 58; translation amended.

168. Lip is a French watch and clock company whose turmoil became emblematic of the conflicts between workers and management in France. The Lip factory, based in Besançon in Eastern France, began to experience financial problems in the late 1960s and early 1970s, and management decided to attempt a factory shutdown. However, after strikes and a highly publicized factory occupation in 1973, Lip became worker-managed. All the fired employees were rehired by March 1974, but the firm was liquidated in the spring of 1976.

169. In 1970, Vaneigem penned "Om Kiruna" to the third and final issue of the journal of the Scandinavian section of the SI, an unsigned text that criticized the Swedish miners' strike in Kiruna. "On Kiruna," in *Situationistisk Revolution* 3, ed. J. V. Martin, October 1970; cf. Debord, *Correspondance*, vol. 4, 365.

170. Vaneigem, *From Wildcat Strike to Total Self-Management*, 46.

171. Vaneigem, 46.

172. A reference to Henri Monnier's 1852 play, *Grandeur et Décadence de Monsieur Joseph Prudhomme*.